2023-2024
CROSSWORD
PUZZEL BOOK

THIS PUZZLE BOOK BELONGS TO

____

____

CROSSWORD PUZZLE

CROSSWORD IS A WORD PUZZLE AND WORD SEARCH GAME. THE GAME'S GOAL IS TO FILL THE SQUARES WITH LETTERS, FORMING WORDS OR PHRASES, BY SOLVING CLUES, WHICH LEAD TO THE ANSWERS. THE CROSSWORD PUZZLES CERTAINLY IS THE BEST WAY TO ENHANCE YOUR IQ AND KEEPS YOUR MIND ACTIVE? CROSSWORD PUZZLES ARE WELL-KNOWN BRAIN GAMES. THEY RE FINEST WAYS OF RELAXATION AND REJUVENATIO.

ONE PUZZLE PER PAGE, VERY EASY TO READ
ALL PUZZLE HAVE SOLUTION AT THE END OF
THE BOOK

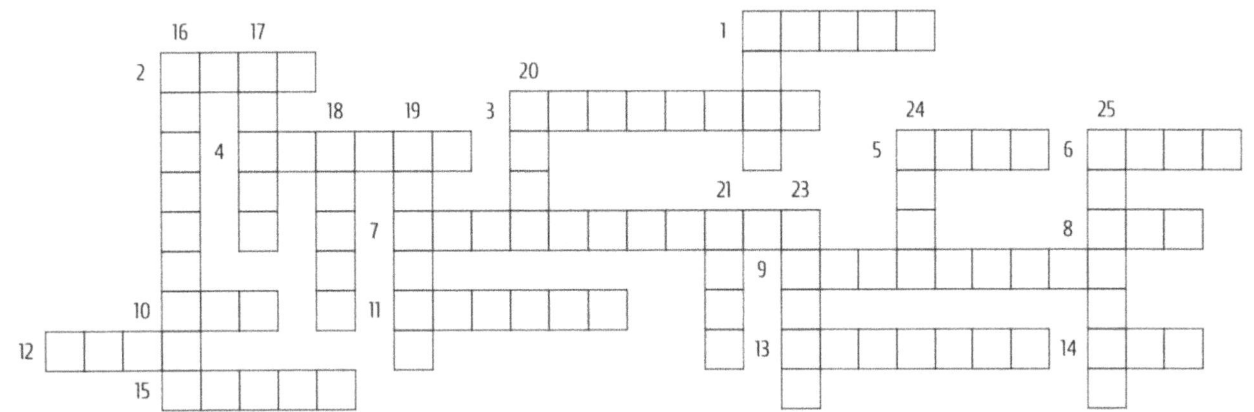

Across

1. find out how heavy (someone or something) is, typically using scales.
2. a word used to describe an action, state, or occurrence, and forming the main part of the predicate of a sentence, such as hear, become, happen.
3. an activity that is natural to or the purpose of a person or thing.
4. take aggressive military action against (a place or enemy forces) with weapons or armed force.
5. inform someone in advance of a possible danger, problem, or other unpleasant situation.
6. keep safe or rescue (someone or something) from harm or danger.
7. A wealthy person
8. come to have (something) receive
9. containing as part of the whole being considered.
10. a large motor vehicle carrying passengers by road, typically one serving the public on a fixed route and for a fare.
11. a very fine slender piece of polished metal with a point at one end and a hole or eye for thread at the other, used in sewing.
12. cause (a space or container) to become full or almost full.
13. giving or ready to give help.
14. past and past participle of sit.
15. not often rarely.

Down

16. a plant or part of a plant used as food, such as a cabbage, potato, turnip, or bean.
17. in a suitable state for an action or situation fully prepared.
18. Give lessons in a subject
19. due to happen or just beginning
20. containing or holding as much or as many as possible having no empty space.
21. a strong, hard magnetic silvery-grey metal, the chemical element of atomic number 26, much used as a material for construction and manufacturing, especially in the form of steel.
22. the fine, soft curly or wavy hair forming the coat of a sheep, goat, or similar animal, especially when shorn and prepared for use in making cloth or yarn.
23. equivalent to the product of two and four one more than seven, or two less than ten-8.
24. expressing the future tense
25. cause one to think that (something) exists or is the case.

Puzzle-01

Puzzle-01

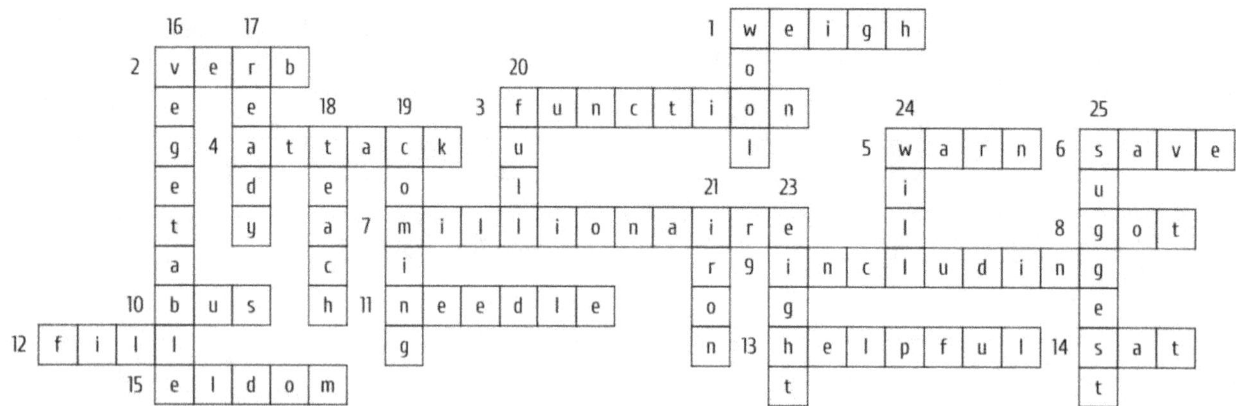

Across

1. find out how heavy (someone or something) is, typically using scales.
2. a word used to describe an action, state, or occurrence, and forming the main part of the predicate of a sentence, such as hear, become, happen.
3. an activity that is natural to or the purpose of a person or thing.
4. take aggressive military action against (a place or enemy forces) with weapons or armed force.
5. inform someone in advance of a possible danger, problem, or other unpleasant situation.
6. keep safe or rescue (someone or something) from harm or danger.
7. A wealthy person
8. come to have (something) receive
9. containing as part of the whole being considered.
10. a large motor vehicle carrying passengers by road, typically one serving the public on a fixed route and for a fare.
11. a very fine slender piece of polished metal with a point at one end and a hole or eye for thread at the other, used in sewing.
12. cause (a space or container) to become full or almost full.
13. giving or ready to give help.
14. past and past participle of sit
15. not often rarely.

Down

16. a plant or part of a plant used as food, such as a cabbage, potato, turnip, or bean.
17. in a suitable state for an action or situation fully prepared.
18. Give lessons in a subject
19. due to happen or just beginning
20. containing or holding as much or as many as possible having no empty space.
21. a strong, hard magnetic silvery-grey metal, the chemical element of atomic number 26, much used as a material for construction and manufacturing, especially in the form of steel.
22. the fine, soft curly or wavy hair forming the coat of a sheep, goat, or similar animal, especially when shorn and prepared for use in making cloth or yarn.
23. equivalent to the product of two and four one more than seven, or two less than ten 8.
24. expressing the future tense
25. cause one to think that (something) exists or is the case.

Across

1. Unhappy or sorry
2. Not guilty of aparticular crime
3. Stopping and starting repeatedly
4. Shaped like a ball or circle
5. Easily deceived
6. Dissolves materials
7. Not physically strong
8. Completely unable to think clearly or behave in a controlled way
9. Happy and positive

Down

10. Fashionable and interesting
11. Said or thought by some people to be the stated bad or illegal thing, although you have no proof
12. Extremely large
13. Very respected
14. Complicated and difficult to solve
15. Ordinary or usual
16. Not bitter or salty
17. Loved very much
18. No water or other liquid in

Puzzle-02

Puzzle-02

Across
1. Unhappy or sorry
2. Not guilty of aparticular crime
3. Stopping and starting repeatedly
4. Shaped like a ball or circle
5. Easily deceived
6. Dissolves materials
7. Not physically strong
8. Completely unable to think clearly or behave in a controlled way
9. Happy and positive

Down
10. Fashionable and interesting
11. Said or thought by some people to be the stated bad or illegal thing, although you have no proof
12. Extremely large
13. Very respected
14. Complicated and difficult to solve
15. Ordinary or usual
16. Not bitter or salty
17. Loved very much
18. No water or other liquid in

Across

1. Not bitter or salty
2. Eager to know a lot
3. Able to be obtained, used, or reached
4. Shaped like a ball or circle
5. Fact that everyone knows
6. Telling not the true

Down

7. Said or thought by some people to be the stated bad or illegal thing, although you have no proof
8. Poor, unsuccessful, the state of being extremely unhappy
9. Ability to do an activity or job well
10. Most excellent, highest quality,
11. Develop
12. Man
13. Complicated and difficult to solve
14. Careful not to attract too much attention

Puzzle-03

Puzzle-03

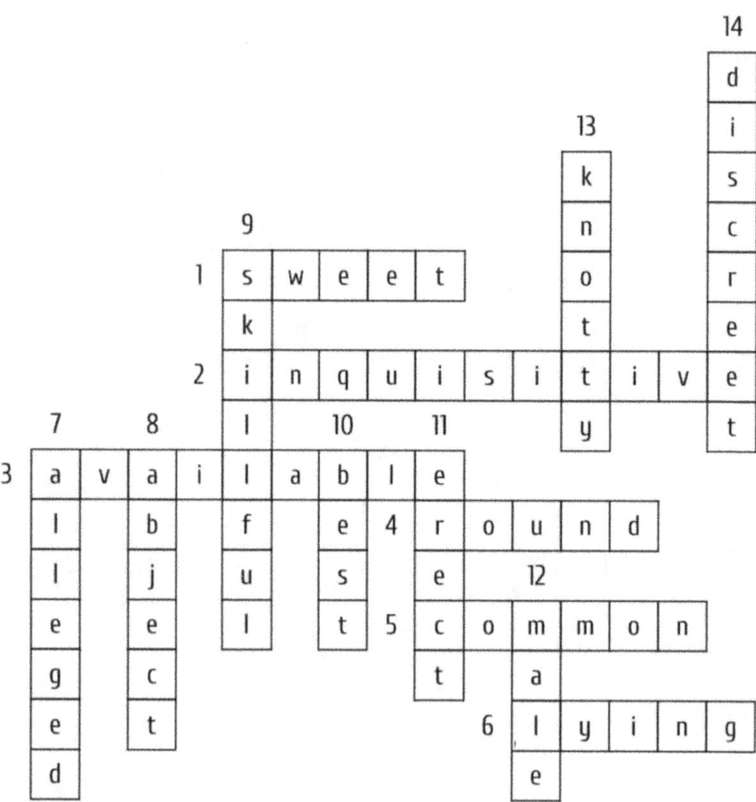

Across
1. Not bitter or salty
2. Eager to know a lot
3. Able to be obtained, used, or reached
4. Shaped like a ball or circle
5. Fact that everyone knows
6. Telling not the true

Down
7. Said or thought by some people to be the stated bad or illegal thing, although you have no proof
8. Poor, unsuccessful, the state of being extremely unhappy
9. Ability to do an activity or job well
10. Most excellent, highest quality,
11. Develop
12. Man
13. Complicated and difficult to solve
14. Careful not to attract too much attention

Across
1. Hing, or activity could harm you
2. Unusual and unexpected
3. Difficult to understand
4. Hard or firm
5. Unacceptable, offensive, violent, or unusual
6. Unhappy or sorry
7. Feeling of energetic interest
8. Shaped like a ball or circle

Down
9. Unkind, cruel, without sympathy
10. Dark and dirty or difficult to see through
11. Loved very much
12. Disappointed discovering the truth
13. Not far away in distance
14. Not in danger or likely to be harmed
15. Develop
16. Ability to do an activity or job well

Puzzle-04

Puzzle-04

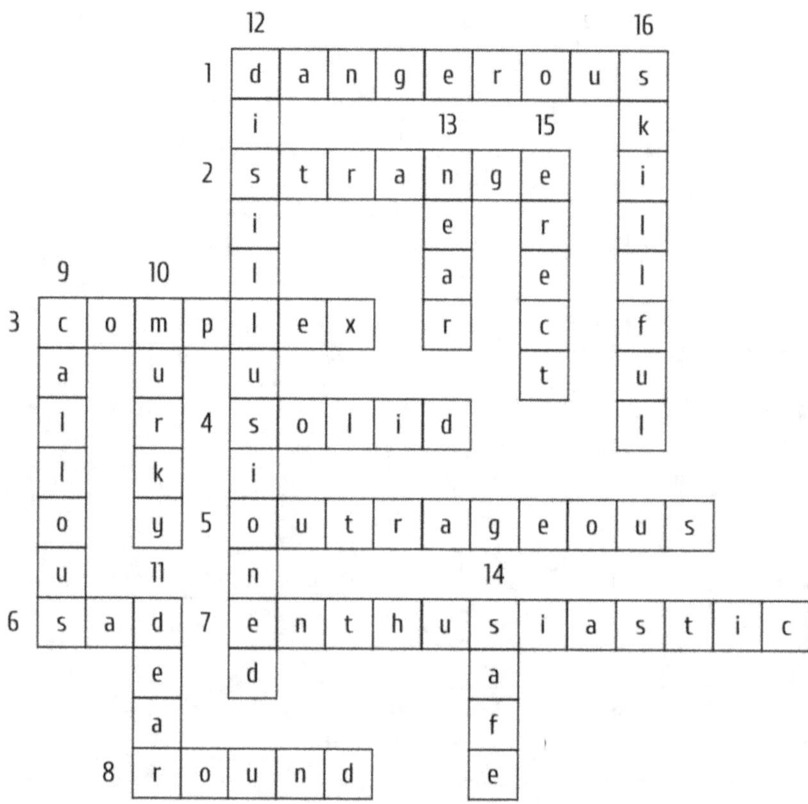

Across
1. Hing, or activity could harm you
2. Unusual and unexpected
3. Difficult to understand
4. Hard or firm
5. Unacceptable, offensive, violent, or unusual
6. Unhappy or sorry
7. Feeling of energetic interest
8. Shaped like a ball or circle

Down
9. Unkind, cruel, without sympathy
10. Dark and dirty or difficult to see through
11. Loved very much
12. Disappointed discovering the truth
13. Not far away in distance
14. Not in danger or likely to be harmed
15. Develop
16. Ability to do an activity or job well

Across

1. Unkind, cruel, without sympathy
2. Dissolves materials
3. Ordinary
4. Develop
5. Gradually and secretly causing harm
6. Complain in an angry way
7. Make something more likely to happen
8. Not bitter or salty

Down

9. Unhappy or sorry
10. Very respected
11. Fact that everyone knows
12. Unwilling to give information
13. Telling not the true
14. Strong and unlikely to break or fail
15. Respecting God
16. Not in danger or likely to be harmed
17. Not far away in distance
18. Not wanting others to know

Puzzle-05

Puzzle-05

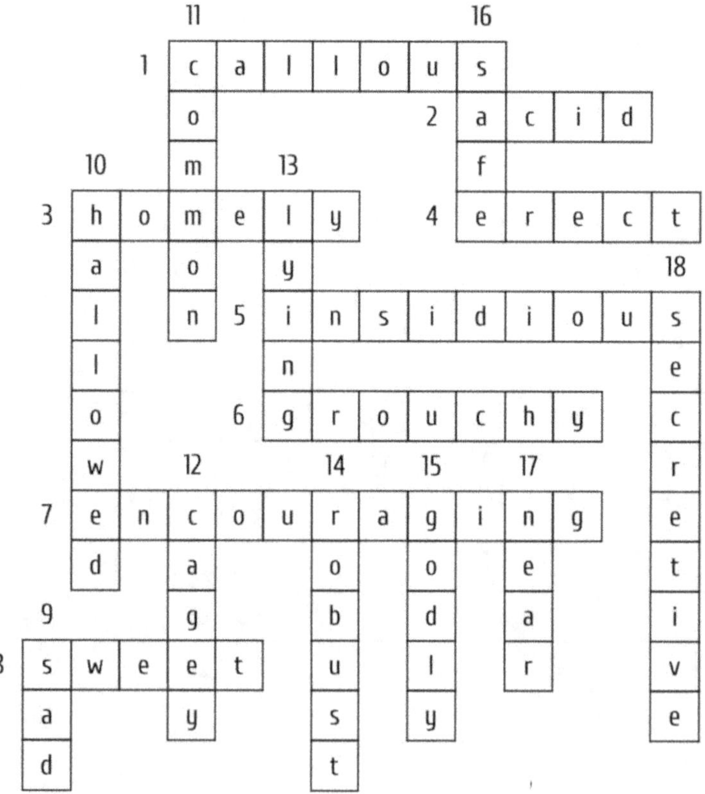

Across
1. Unkind, cruel, without sympathy
2. Dissolves materials
3. Ordinary
4. Develop
5. Gradually and secretly causing harm
6. Complain in an angry way
7. Make something more likely to happen
8. Not bitter or salty

Down
9. Unhappy or sorry
10. Very respected
11. Fact that everyone knows
12. Unwilling to give information
13. Telling not the true
14. Strong and unlikely to break or fail
15. Respecting God
16. Not in danger or likely to be harmed
17. Not far away in distance
18. Not wanting others to know

Across

1. Very happy
2. Containing, tasting of, or similar to nuts
3. Shaped like a ball or circle
4. Develop
5. Careful not to attract too much attention
6. Without a home
7. Loved very much
8. Ordinary or usual

Down

9. Feel slightly drunk
10. Dark and dirty or difficult to see through
11. Telling not the true
12. Happening or done quickly and without warning
13. Unacceptable, offensive, violent, or unusual
14. Not armed
15. Having a lot of energy
16. Happy or grateful because of something

Puzzle-06

Puzzle-06

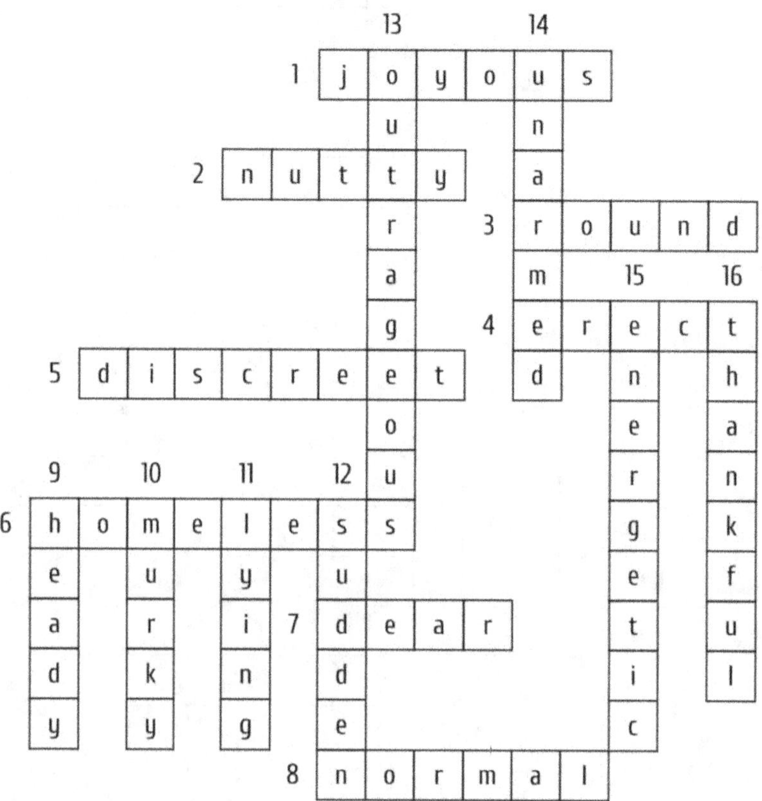

Across
1. Very happy
2. Containing, tasting of, or similar to nuts
3. Shaped like a ball or circle
4. Develop
5. Careful not to attract too much attention
6. Without a home
7. Loved very much
8. Ordinary or usual

Down
9. Feel slightly drunk
10. Dark and dirty or difficult to see through
11. Telling not the true
12. Happening or done quickly and without warning
13. Unacceptable, offensive, violent, or unusual
14. Not armed
15. Having a lot of energy
16. Happy or grateful because of something

Across

1. Not far away in distance
2. Not the same
3. Ability to do an activity or job well
4. Happening or done quickly and without warning
5. Shaped like a ball or circle
6. Able to stretch
7. Limited to only one person
8. No water or other liquid in
9. Showing much knowledge

Down

10. Careful not to attract too much attention
11. Causing pain intentionally
12. Unhappy or sorry
13. Not bitter or salty
14. Containing, tasting of, or similar to nuts
15. Poor, unsuccessful, the state of being extremely unhappy
16. Rounded in a pleasant and attractive way

Puzzle-07

Puzzle-07

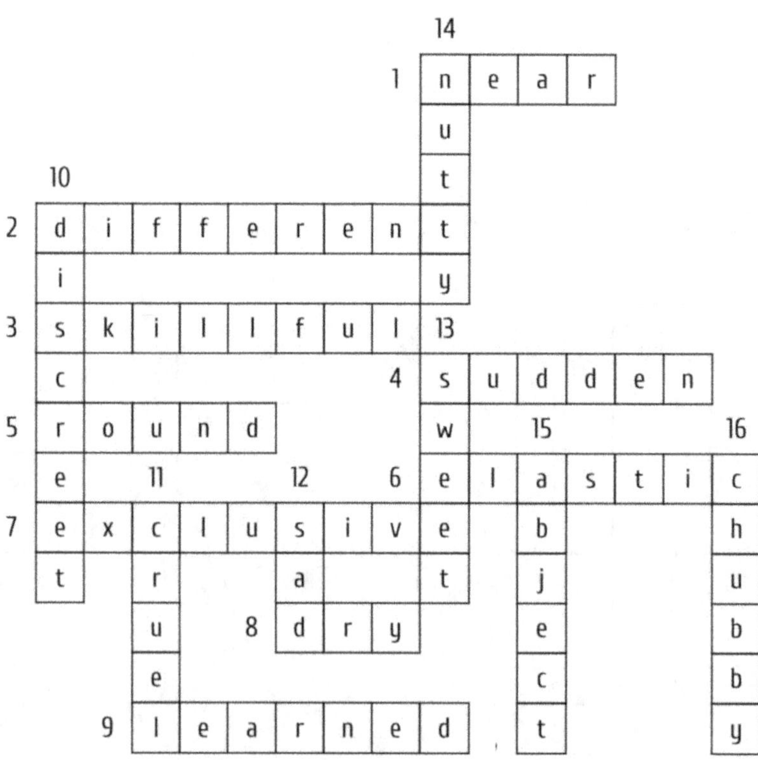

Across
1. Not far away in distance
2. Not the same
3. Ability to do an activity or job well
4. Happening or done quickly and without warning
5. Shaped like a ball or circle
6. Able to stretch
7. Limited to only one person
8. No water or other liquid in
9. Showing much knowledge

Down
10. Careful not to attract too much attention
11. Causing pain intentionally
12. Unhappy or sorry
13. Not bitter or salty
14. Containing, tasting of, or similar to nuts
15. Poor, unsuccessful, the state of being extremely unhappy
16. Rounded in a pleasant and attractive way

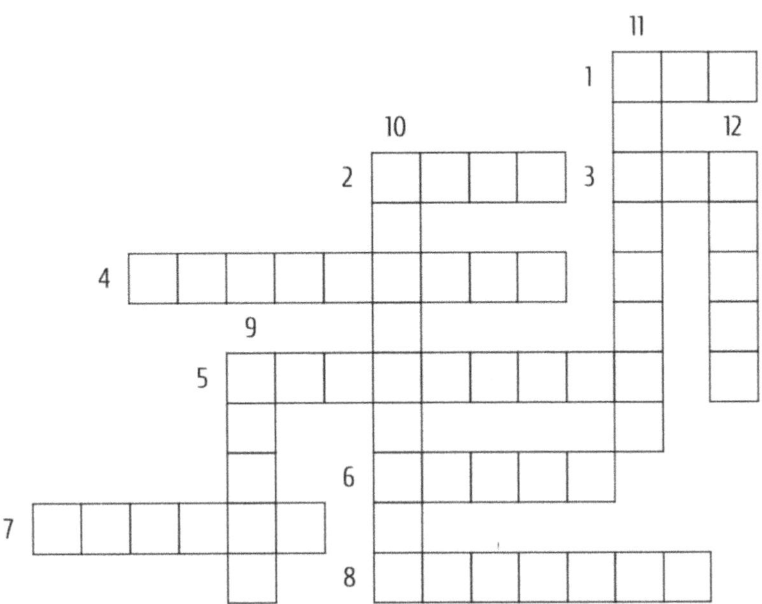

Across

1. No water or other liquid in
2. Dissolves materials
3. Unhappy or sorry
4. Detestable, repugnant, repulsive, morally very bad
5. Intentionally choosing some things and not others
6. Unhappy because you have nothing to do
7. Happening or done quickly and without warning
8. Able to stretch

Down

9. Not bitter or salty
10. Accepted, accept something
11. Careful not to attract too much attention
12. Drinking too much alcohol

Puzzle-08

Puzzle-08

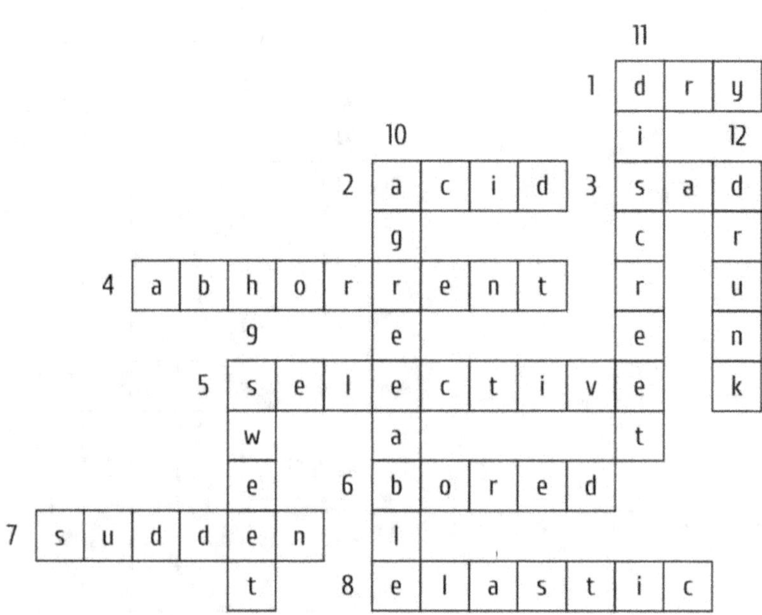

Across

1. No water or other liquid in
2. Dissolves materials
3. Unhappy or sorry
4. Detestable, repugnant, repulsive, morally very bad
5. Intentionally choosing some things and not others
6. Unhappy because you have nothing to do
7. Happening or done quickly and without warning
8. Able to stretch

Down

9. Not bitter or salty
10. Accepted, accept something
11. Careful not to attract too much attention
12. Drinking too much alcohol

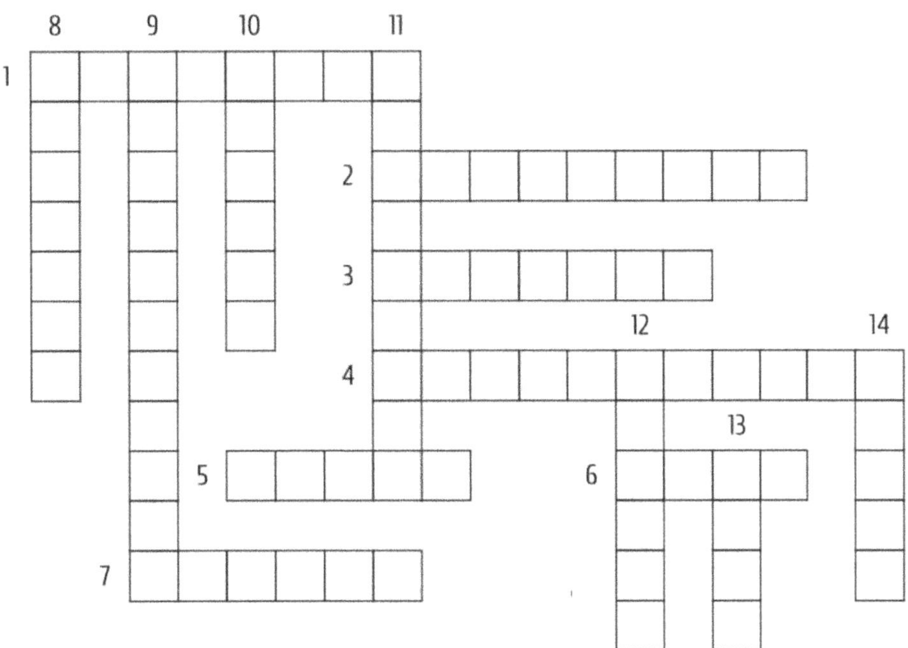

Across

1. Glue
2. Eager to fight or argue
3. Not armed
4. Eager to know a lot
5. Not bitter or salty
6. Loved very much
7. Ordinary or usual

Down

8. Said or thought by some people to be the stated bad or illegal thing, although you have no proof
9. Trying to seem very important
10. Immediately after the first and before any others
11. Limited to only one person
12. Happening or done quickly and without warning
13. Dissolves materials
14. Develop

Puzzle-09

Puzzle-09

Across
1. Glue
2. Eager to fight or argue
3. Not armed
4. Eager to know a lot
5. Not bitter or salty
6. Loved very much
7. Ordinary or usual

Down
8. Said or thought by some people to be the stated bad or illegal thing, although you have no proof
9. Trying to seem very important
10. Immediately after the first and before any others
11. Limited to only one person
12. Happening or done quickly and without warning
13. Dissolves materials
14. Develop

Across

1. Not far away in distance
2. Without a home
3. Drinking too much alcohol
4. Fashionable and interesting
5. Unhappy or sorry
6. Not in danger or likely to be harmed
7. Unpleasant and causing difficulties or harm, evil, low quality, not acceptable
8. Nothing more than
9. Careful not to attract too much attention
10. Ordinary or usual

Down

11. Happening or done quickly and without warning
12. Feel slightly drunk
13. Beautiful, powerful, or causing great admiration and respect
14. Easily deceived
15. Not bitter or salty
16. Gradually and secretly causing harm
17. Having a pleasant smell
18. Develop

Puzzle-10

Puzzle-10

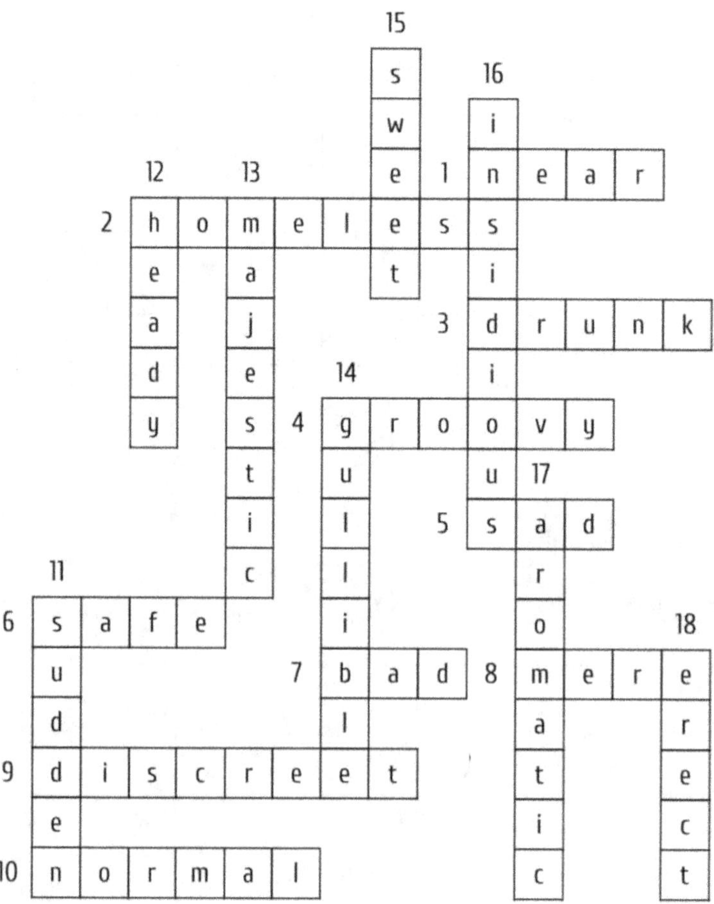

Across

1. Not far away in distance
2. Without a home
3. Drinking too much alcohol
4. Fashionable and interesting
5. Unhappy or sorry
6. Not in danger or likely to be harmed
7. Unpleasant and causing difficulties or harm, evil, low quality, not acceptable
8. Nothing more than
9. Careful not to attract too much attention
10. Ordinary or usual

Down

11. Happening or done quickly and without warning
12. Feel slightly drunk
13. Beautiful, powerful, or causing great admiration and respect
14. Easily deceived
15. Not bitter or salty
16. Gradually and secretly causing harm
17. Having a pleasant smell
18. Develop

Across

1. Not far away in distance
2. Losing against someone
3. Happy or grateful because of something
4. No water or other liquid in
5. Not guilty of aparticular crime
6. Officer

Down

7. Containing, tasting of, or similar to nuts
8. Extremely surprising, very good, extremely surprised
9. Not the same
10. Telling not the true
11. Dissolves materials
12. Happening or done quickly and without warning

Puzzle-11

Puzzle-11

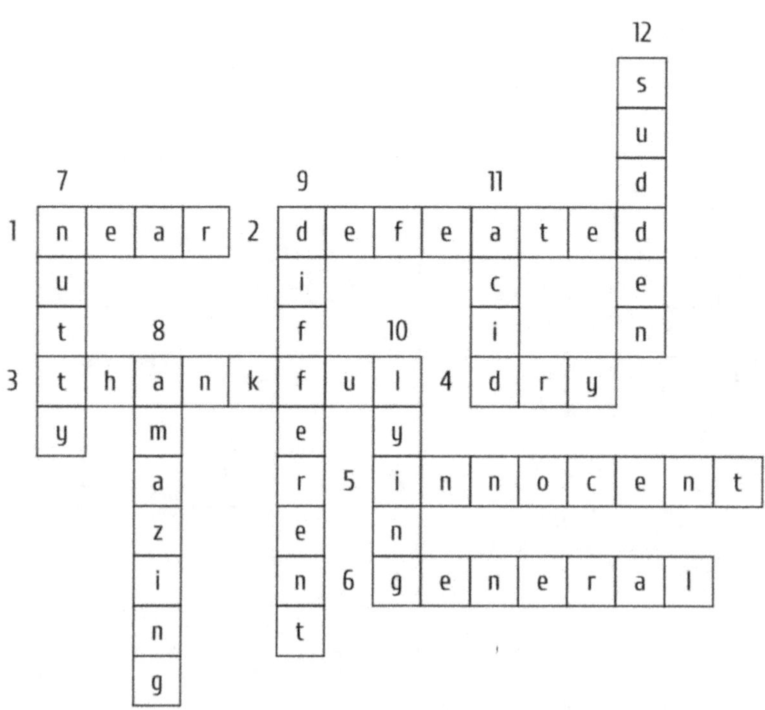

Across
1. Not far away in distance
2. Losing against someone
3. Happy or grateful because of something
4. No water or other liquid in
5. Not guilty of aparticular crime
6. Officer

Down
7. Containing, tasting of, or similar to nuts
8. Extremely surprising, very good, extremely surprised
9. Not the same
10. Telling not the true
11. Dissolves materials
12. Happening or done quickly and without warning

Across

1. Trying to seem very important
2. Behave like adults
3. Develop
4. At the same height
5. Not far away in distance
6. Not in danger or likely to be harmed
7. Abnormal, deviant, different
8. Attractive or pleasant

Down

9. Large in size or amount
10. Without a home
11. Coming before all others
12. Not armed
13. Inside the body
14. Poor, unsuccessful, the state of being extremely unhappy
15. Complicated and difficult to solve

Puzzle-12

Puzzle-12

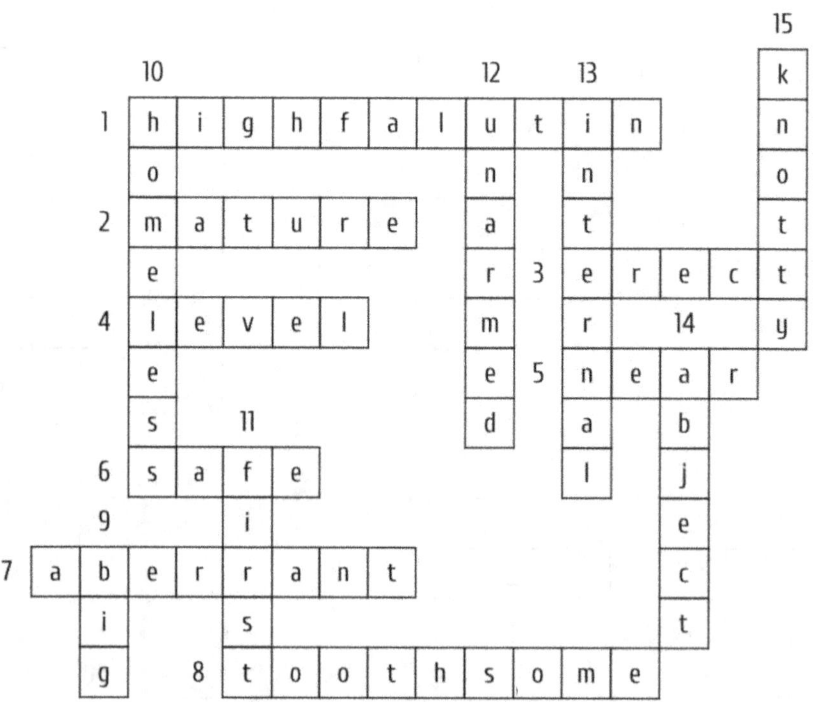

Across
1. Trying to seem very important
2. Behave like adults
3. Develop
4. At the same height
5. Not far away in distance
6. Not in danger or likely to be harmed
7. Abnormal, deviant, different
8. Attractive or pleasant

Down
9. Large in size or amount
10. Without a home
11. Coming before all others
12. Not armed
13. Inside the body
14. Poor, unsuccessful, the state of being extremely unhappy
15. Complicated and difficult to solve

Across

1. Having a lot of energy
2. On or onto a ship, aircraft, bus, or train
3. At the same height
4. Not in danger or likely to be harmed
5. Attractive in appearance
6. Containing, tasting of, or similar to nuts
7. Not dirty
8. Level and smooth

Down

9. Ordinary or usual
10. Feeling of energetic interest
11. Telling not the true
12. Limited to only one person
13. Officer
14. Not far away in distance
15. Revealing
16. Excited, interested, enthusiastic
17. Unkind, cruel, without sympathy
18. Happy or grateful because of something
19. Often forgetting things

Puzzle-13

Puzzle-13

Across
1. Having a lot of energy
2. On or onto a ship, aircraft, bus, or train
3. At the same height
4. Not in danger or likely to be harmed
5. Attractive in appearance
6. Containing, tasting of, or similar to nuts
7. Not dirty
8. Level and smooth

Down
9. Ordinary or usual
10. Feeling of energetic interest
11. Telling not the true
12. Limited to only one person
13. Officer
14. Not far away in distance
15. Revealing
16. Excited, interested, enthusiastic
17. Unkind, cruel, without sympathy
18. Happy or grateful because of something
19. Often forgetting things

Across

1. Unhappy or sorry
2. Attractive, appealing, lovely, charming, and easily loved
3. Develop
4. Hard or firm
5. Disapproving, wishing to fight or argue
6. Drinking too much alcohol
7. Dissolves materials
8. Containing, tasting of, or similar to nuts

Down

9. The color of chocolate
10. Easily deceived
11. Respecting God
12. Abnormal, deviant, different
13. Not far away in distance
14. Rounded in a pleasant and attractive way
15. Happening or done quickly and without warning
16. Careful not to attract too much attention
17. Loved very much

Puzzle-14

Puzzle-14

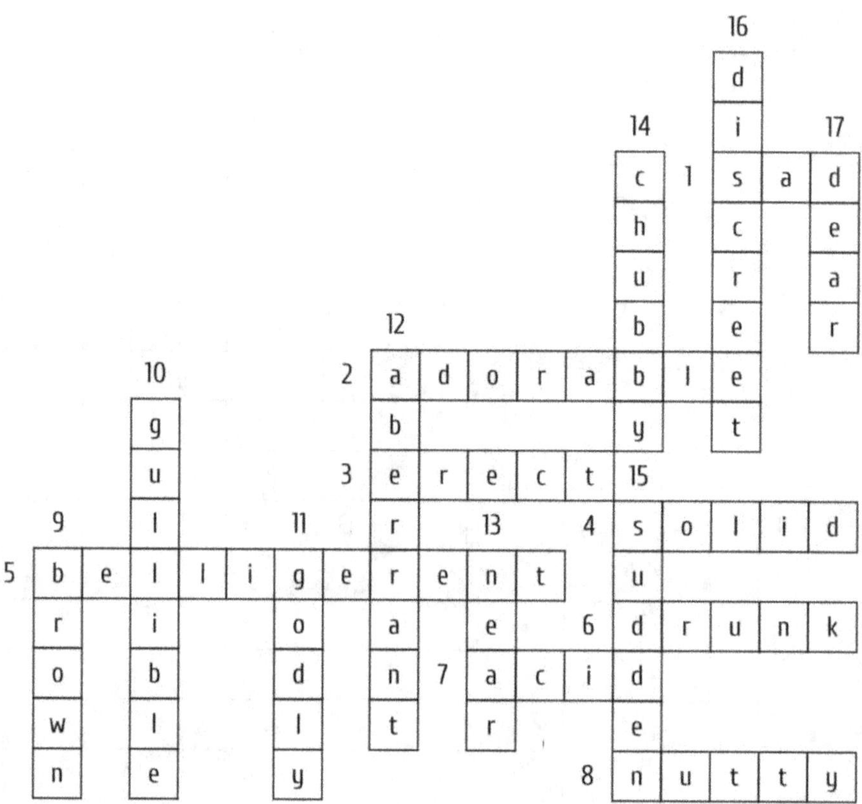

Across
1. Unhappy or sorry
2. Attractive, appealing, lovely, charming, and easily loved
3. Develop
4. Hard or firm
5. Disapproving, wishing to fight or argue
6. Drinking too much alcohol
7. Dissolves materials
8. Containing, tasting of, or similar to nuts

Down
9. The color of chocolate
10. Easily deceived
11. Respecting God
12. Abnormal, deviant, different
13. Not far away in distance
14. Rounded in a pleasant and attractive way
15. Happening or done quickly and without warning
16. Careful not to attract too much attention
17. Loved very much

Across

1. Ordinary or usual
2. Attractive or pleasant
3. Beautiful, powerful, or causing great admiration and respect
4. Revealing
5. Not armed

Down

6. Complicated and difficult to solve
7. Unacceptable, offensive, violent, or unusual
8. Extremely ugly or bad
9. Gigantic prehistoric animal
10. No water or other liquid in
11. Telling not the true
12. Containing, tasting of, or similar to nuts
13. Not far away in distance

Puzzle-15

Puzzle-15

Across
1. Ordinary or usual
2. Attractive or pleasant
3. Beautiful, powerful, or causing great admiration and respect
4. Revealing
5. Not armed

Down
6. Complicated and difficult to solve
7. Unacceptable, offensive, violent, or unusual
8. Extremely ugly or bad
9. Gigantic prehistoric animal
10. No water or other liquid in
11. Telling not the true
12. Containing, tasting of, or similar to nuts
13. Not far away in distance

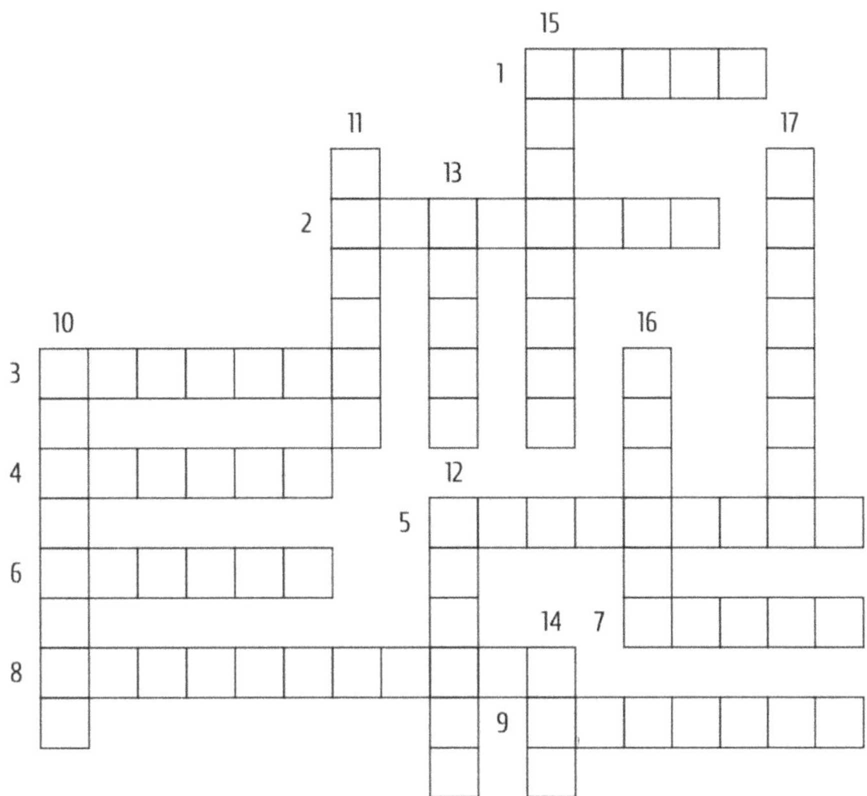

Across

1. Unkind, cruel
2. Not clear and having no form
3. Refusing to obey
4. Rightened or worried
5. Grand very large
6. Strong and unlikely to break or fail
7. Containing, tasting of, or similar to nuts
8. Able to produce the intended result
9. Said or thought by some people to be the stated bad or illegal thing, although you have no proof

Down

10. Careful not to attract too much attention
11. Complicated and difficult to solve
12. Fashionable and interesting
13. Unhappy because you have nothing to do
14. Unhappy or sorry
15. Very respected
16. Happening or done quickly and without warning
17. Without a home

Puzzle-16

Puzzle-16

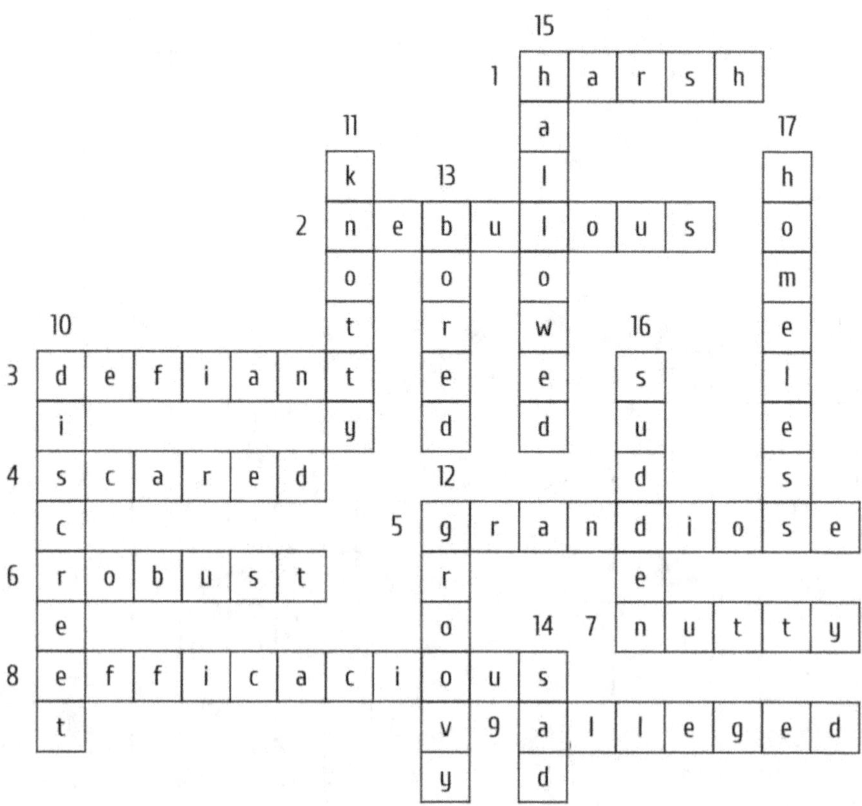

Across
1. Unkind, cruel
2. Not clear and having no form
3. Refusing to obey
4. Rightened or worried
5. Grand very large
6. Strong and unlikely to break or fail
7. Containing, tasting of, or similar to nuts
8. Able to produce the intended result
9. Said or thought by some people to be the stated bad or illegal thing, although you have no proof

Down
10. Careful not to attract too much attention
11. Complicated and difficult to solve
12. Fashionable and interesting
13. Unhappy because you have nothing to do
14. Unhappy or sorry
15. Very respected
16. Happening or done quickly and without warning
17. Without a home

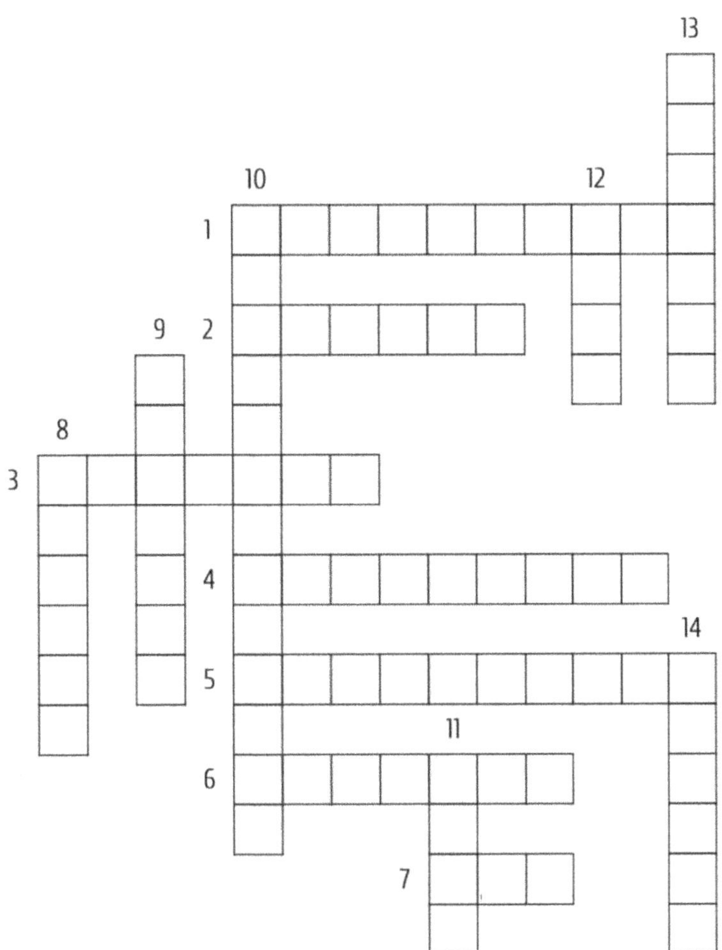

Across

1. Very pleasant
2. Not difficult
3. Difficult to understand
4. Not wanting others to know
5. Unacceptable, offensive, violent, or unusual
6. Attractive in appearance
7. Extremely cold

Down

8. Fact that everyone knows
9. Extremely large
10. Disappointed discovering the truth
11. Dissolves materials
12. Level and smooth
13. Unkind, cruel, without sympathy
14. Immediately after the first and before any others

Puzzle-17

Puzzle-17

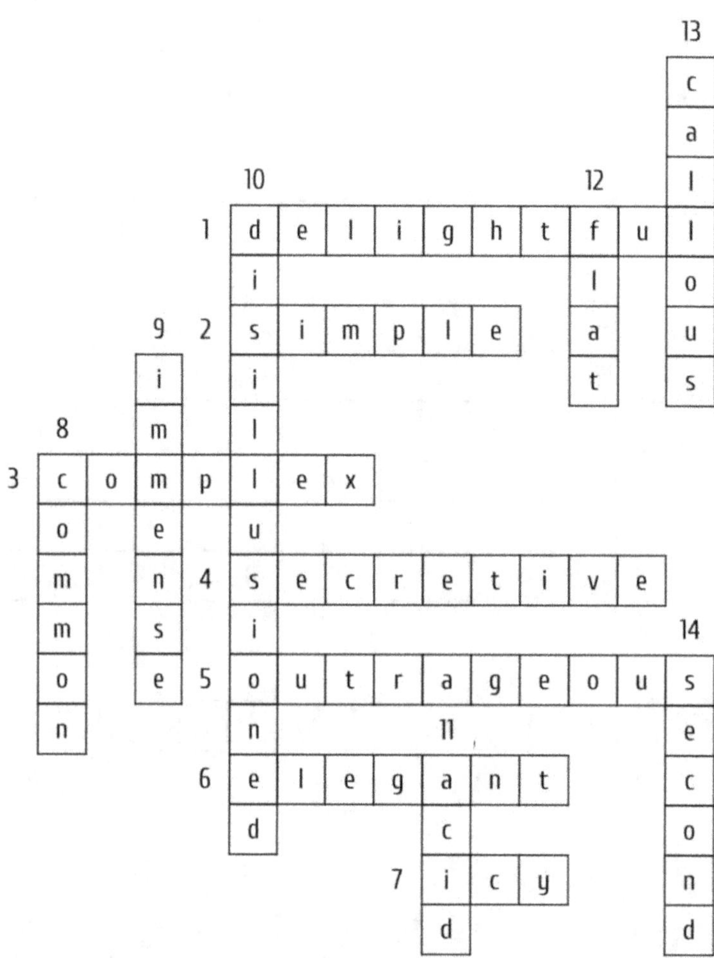

Across
1. Very pleasant
2. Not difficult
3. Difficult to understand
4. Not wanting others to know
5. Unacceptable, offensive, violent, or unusual
6. Attractive in appearance
7. Extremely cold

Down
8. Fact that everyone knows
9. Extremely large
10. Disappointed discovering the truth
11. Dissolves materials
12. Level and smooth
13. Unkind, cruel, without sympathy
14. Immediately after the first and before any others

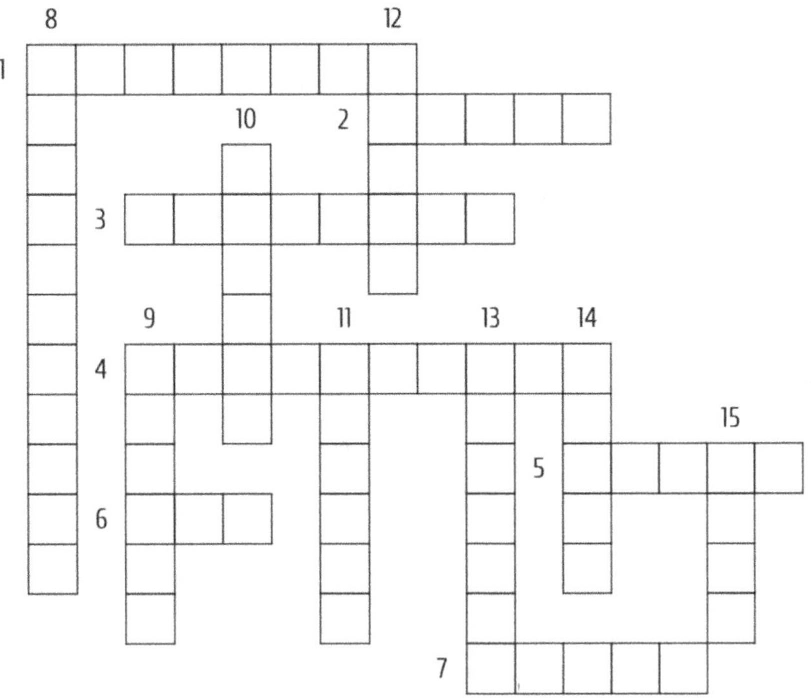

Across

1. Without a home
2. Complete or not divided
3. Not guilty of aparticular crime
4. Making you feel pleased by providing what you need or want
5. Drinking too much alcohol
6. No water or other liquid in
7. Not dirty

Down

8. Trying to seem very important
9. Happening or done quickly and without warning
10. Complicated and difficult to solve
11. Rightened or worried
12. Not bitter or salty
13. A foolish idea
14. Respecting God
15. Not far away in distance

Puzzle-18

Puzzle-18

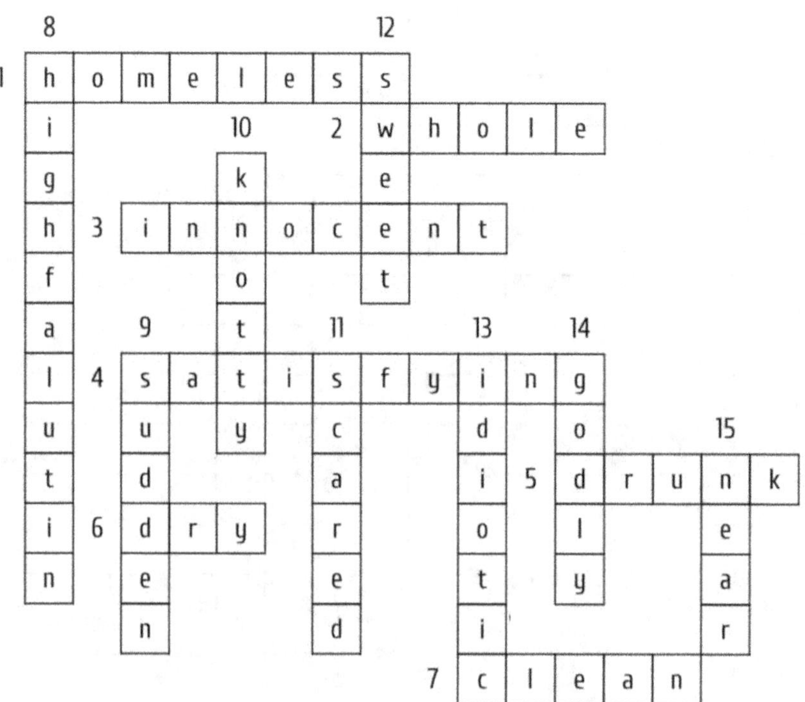

Across
1. Without a home
2. Complete or not divided
3. Not guilty of aparticular crime
4. Making you feel pleased by providing what you need or want
5. Drinking too much alcohol
6. No water or other liquid in
7. Not dirty

Down
8. Trying to seem very important
9. Happening or done quickly and without warning
10. Complicated and difficult to solve
11. Rightened or worried
12. Not bitter or salty
13. A foolish idea
14. Respecting God
15. Not far away in distance

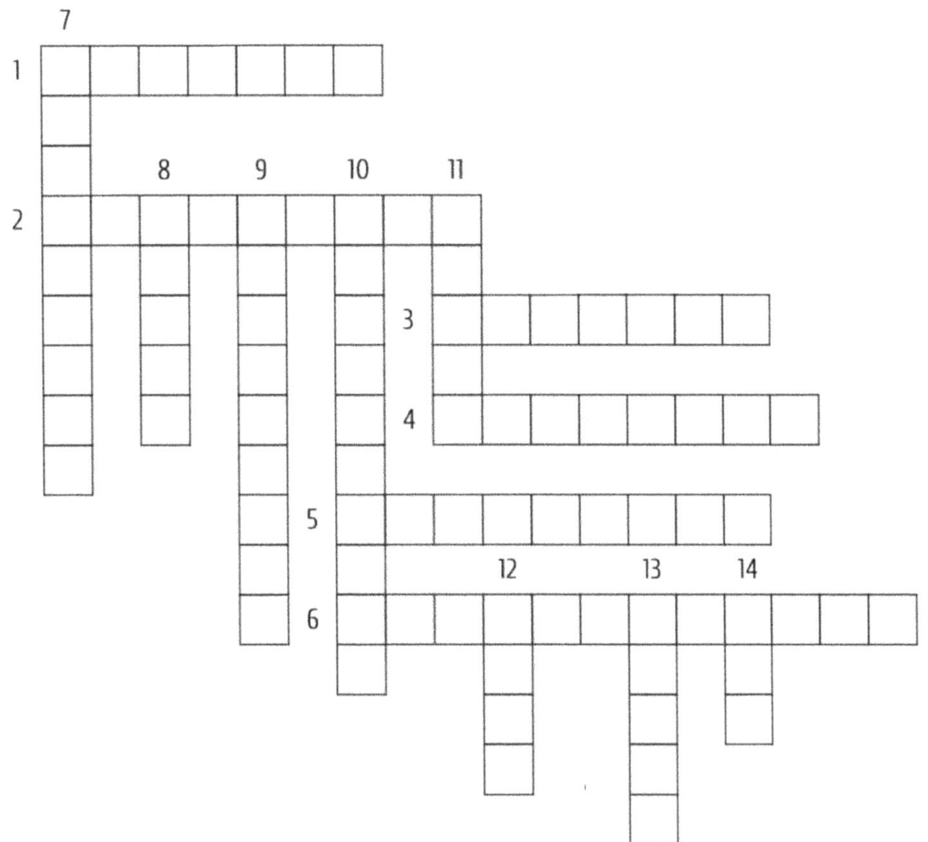

Across

1. Officer
2. Morally correct
3. Showing much knowledge
4. Completely unable to think clearly or behave in a controlled way
5. Having a lot of energy
6. Not excited

Down

7. Habit of talking a lot
8. Respecting God
9. Attractive or pleasant
10. Unacceptable, offensive, violent, or unusual
11. Hard or firm
12. Not far away in distance
13. Shaped like a ball or circle
14. Unhappy or sorry

Puzzle-19

Puzzle-19

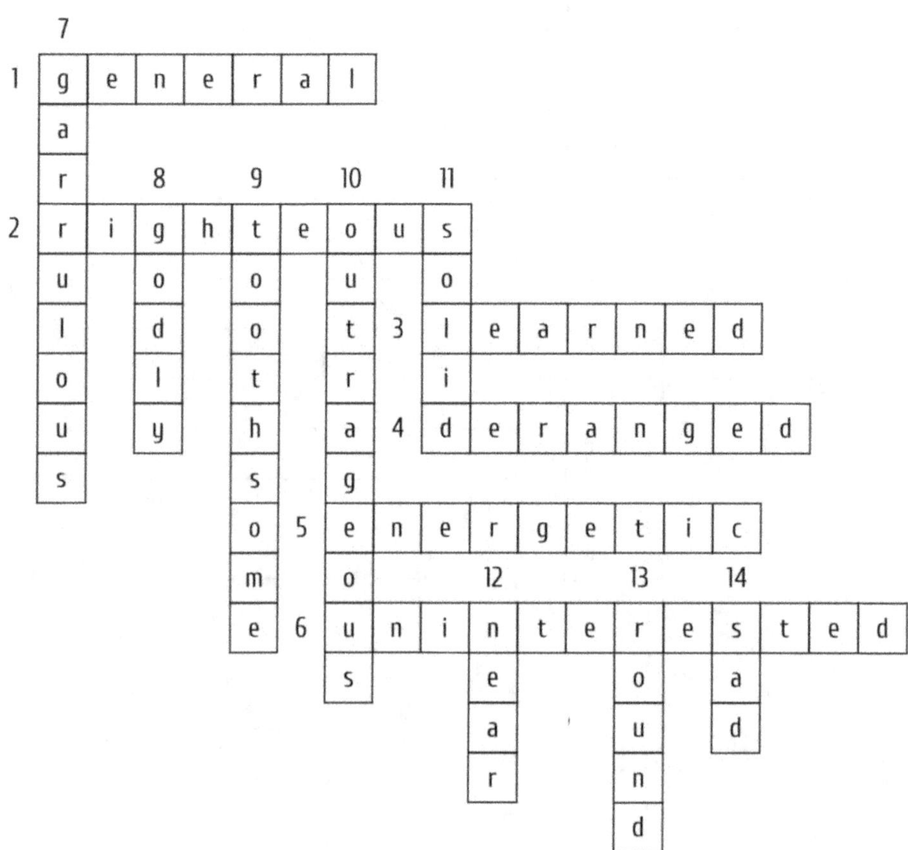

Across
1. Officer
2. Morally correct
3. Showing much knowledge
4. Completely unable to think clearly or behave in a controlled way
5. Having a lot of energy
6. Not excited

Down
7. Habit of talking a lot
8. Respecting God
9. Attractive or pleasant
10. Unacceptable, offensive, violent, or unusual
11. Hard or firm
12. Not far away in distance
13. Shaped like a ball or circle
14. Unhappy or sorry

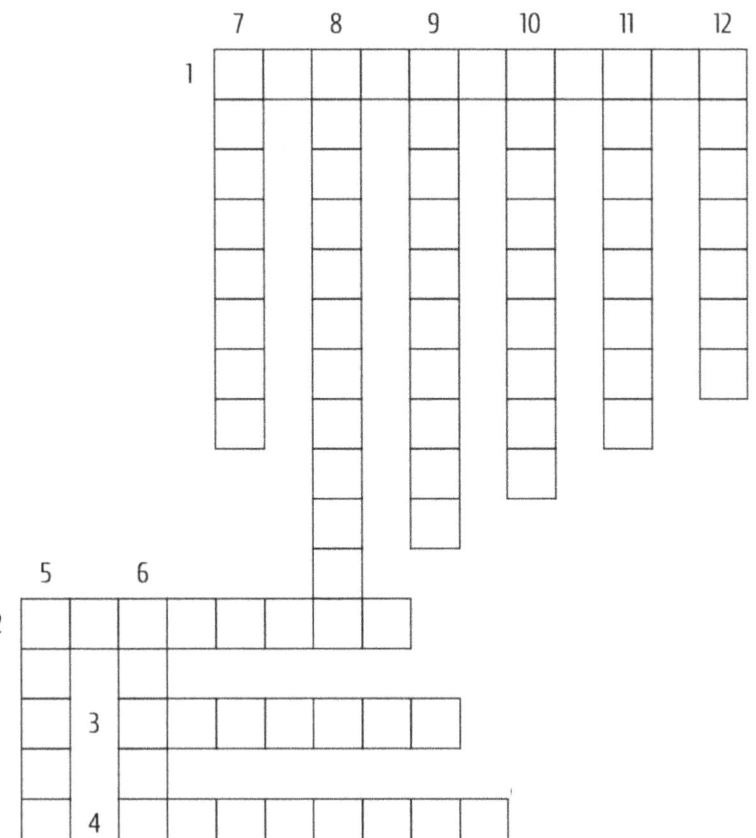

Across
1. Eager to know a lot
2. Careful not to attract too much attention
3. Showing much knowledge
4. Completely unable to think clearly or behave in a controlled way

Down
5. Drinking too much alcohol
6. Hard or firm
7. Not guilty of aparticular crime
8. Not certain, or wrong in some way
9. Impossible to defeat
10. Gradually and secretly causing harm
11. Inside the body
12. Able to stretch

Puzzle-20

Puzzle-20

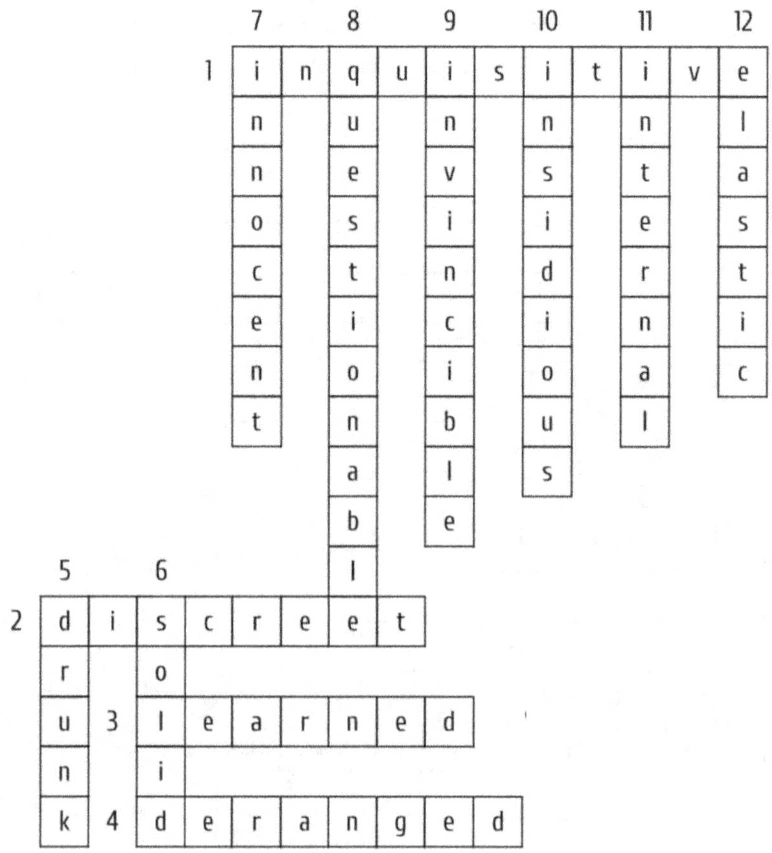

Across

1. Eager to know a lot
2. Careful not to attract too much attention
3. Showing much knowledge
4. Completely unable to think clearly or behave in a controlled way

Down

5. Drinking too much alcohol
6. Hard or firm
7. Not guilty of aparticular crime
8. Not certain, or wrong in some way
9. Impossible to defeat
10. Gradually and secretly causing harm
11. Inside the body
12. Able to stretch

Across

1. Beautiful, powerful, or causing great admiration and respect
2. Ordinary or usual
3. Careful not to attract too much attention
4. Damaged
5. Accepted, accept something
6. No water or other liquid in
7. Not in danger or likely to be harmed

Down

8. Not the same
9. Ability to do an activity or job well
10. Nothing more than
11. Strong and unlikely to break or fail
12. Young person
13. Dissolves materials
14. Immediately after the first and before any others
15. Morally correct
16. Impossible to defeat
17. Said or thought by some people to be the stated bad or illegal thing, although you have no proof
18. Showing much knowledge

Puzzle-21

Puzzle-21

Across
1. Beautiful, powerful, or causing great admiration and respect
2. Ordinary or usual
3. Careful not to attract too much attention
4. Damaged
5. Accepted, accept something
6. No water or other liquid in
7. Not in danger or likely to be harmed

Down
8. Not the same
9. Ability to do an activity or job well
10. Nothing more than
11. Strong and unlikely to break or fail
12. Young person
13. Dissolves materials
14. Immediately after the first and before any others
15. Morally correct
16. Impossible to defeat
17. Said or thought by some people to be the stated bad or illegal thing, although you have no proof
18. Showing much knowledge

Across

1. Not far away in distance
2. Very pleasant
3. Not bitter or salty
4. Morally correct
5. Causing pain intentionally
6. Shaped like a ball or circle
7. Attractive in appearance
8. No water or other liquid in

Down

9. Unwilling to give information
10. Careful not to attract too much attention
11. Containing, tasting of, or similar to nuts
12. Complicated and difficult to solve
13. Not armed
14. Happening or done quickly and without warning

Puzzle-22

Puzzle-22

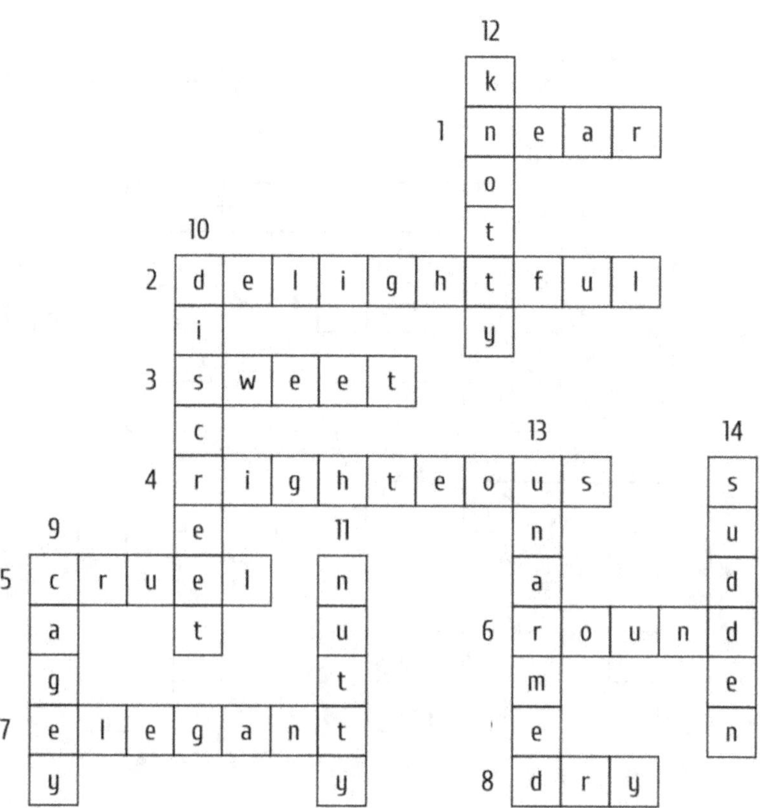

Across
1. Not far away in distance
2. Very pleasant
3. Not bitter or salty
4. Morally correct
5. Causing pain intentionally
6. Shaped like a ball or circle
7. Attractive in appearance
8. No water or other liquid in

Down
9. Unwilling to give information
10. Careful not to attract too much attention
11. Containing, tasting of, or similar to nuts
12. Complicated and difficult to solve
13. Not armed
14. Happening or done quickly and without warning

Across

1. Easily deceived
2. Poor, unsuccessful, the state of being extremely unhappy
3. Not far away in distance
4. Loved very much
5. Man
6. Ordinary or usual
7. Fact that everyone knows

Down

8. Respecting God
9. Telling not the true
10. A foolish idea
11. Showing much knowledge
12. Having a lot of energy
13. Relating to love or a close loving relationship
14. Complicated and difficult to solve

Puzzle-23

Puzzle-23

Across
1. Easily deceived
2. Poor, unsuccessful, the state of being extremely unhappy
3. Not far away in distance
4. Loved very much
5. Man
6. Ordinary or usual
7. Fact that everyone knows

Down
8. Respecting God
9. Telling not the true
10. A foolish idea
11. Showing much knowledge
12. Having a lot of energy
13. Relating to love or a close loving relationship
14. Complicated and difficult to solve

Across
1. Ordinary or usual
2. Nothing more than
3. Not excited
4. Boring

Down
5. Man
6. Shaped like a ball or circle
7. Strong and unlikely to break or fail
8. Damaged
9. Containing, tasting of, or similar to nuts
10. Relating to love or a close loving relationship
11. Ability to do an activity or job well
12. Attractive in appearance

Puzzle-24

Puzzle-24

Across
1. Ordinary or usual
2. Nothing more than
3. Not excited
4. Boring

Down
5. Man
6. Shaped like a ball or circle
7. Strong and unlikely to break or fail
8. Damaged
9. Containing, tasting of, or similar to nuts
10. Relating to love or a close loving relationship
11. Ability to do an activity or job well
12. Attractive in appearance

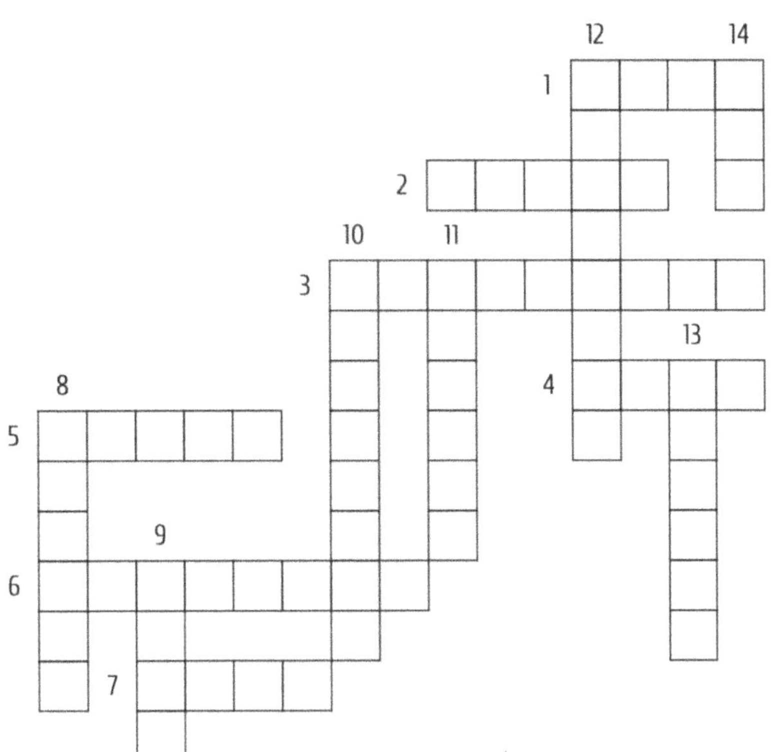

Across

1. Dissolves materials
2. Not bitter or salty
3. Detestable, repugnant, repulsive, morally very bad
4. Not far away in distance
5. Hard or firm
6. Careful not to attract too much attention
7. Level and smooth

Down

8. Happening or done quickly and without warning
9. Not in danger or likely to be harmed
10. Excited, interested, enthusiastic
11. Ordinary
12. Abnormal, deviant, different
13. On or onto a ship, aircraft, bus, or train
14. No water or other liquid in

Puzzle-25

Puzzle-25

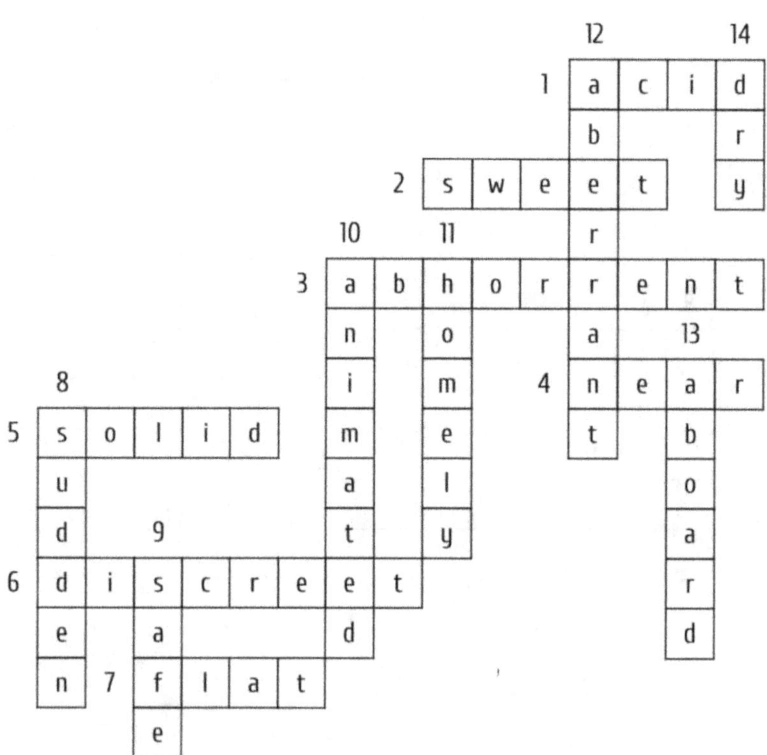

Across
1. Dissolves materials
2. Not bitter or salty
3. Detestable, repugnant, repulsive, morally very bad
4. Not far away in distance
5. Hard or firm
6. Careful not to attract too much attention
7. Level and smooth

Down
8. Happening or done quickly and without warning
9. Not in danger or likely to be harmed
10. Excited, interested, enthusiastic
11. Ordinary
12. Abnormal, deviant, different
13. On or onto a ship, aircraft, bus, or train
14. No water or other liquid in

Across
1. No water or other liquid in
2. Easy to understand
3. Officer
4. Not clear and having no form
5. On or onto a ship, aircraft, bus, or train
6. Relating to love or a close loving relationship
7. Without a home
8. Not smooth
9. Telling not the true
10. Drinking too much alcohol
11. Happening or done quickly and without warning

Down
12. Shaped like a ball or circle
13. Fact that everyone knows
14. Complicated and difficult to solve
15. Rounded in a pleasant and attractive way
16. Fashionable and interesting
17. Unhappy or sorry
18. Hard or firm
19. Careful not to attract too much attention
20. Loved very much

Puzzle-26

Puzzle-26

Across
1. No water or other liquid in
2. Easy to understand
3. Officer
4. Not clear and having no form
5. On or onto a ship, aircraft, bus, or train
6. Relating to love or a close loving relationship
7. Without a home
8. Not smooth
9. Telling not the true
10. Drinking too much alcohol
11. Happening or done quickly and without warning

Down
12. Shaped like a ball or circle
13. Fact that everyone knows
14. Complicated and difficult to solve
15. Rounded in a pleasant and attractive way
16. Fashionable and interesting
17. Unhappy or sorry
18. Hard or firm
19. Careful not to attract too much attention
20. Loved very much

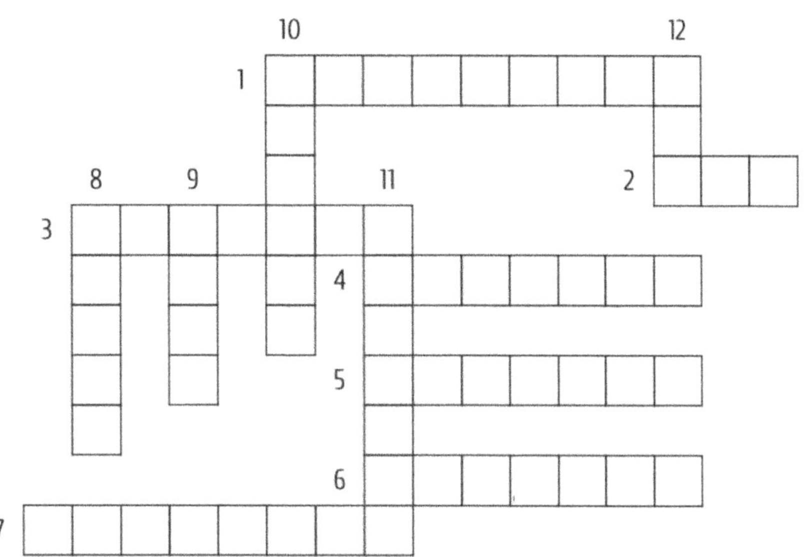

Across

1. Habit of talking a lot
2. No water or other liquid in
3. Gigantic prehistoric animal
4. Extremely large
5. Able to stretch
6. Not armed
7. Without a home

Down

8. Dark and dirty or difficult to see through
9. Nothing more than
10. Fashionable and interesting
11. Extremely ugly or bad
12. Unhappy or sorry

Puzzle-27

Puzzle-27

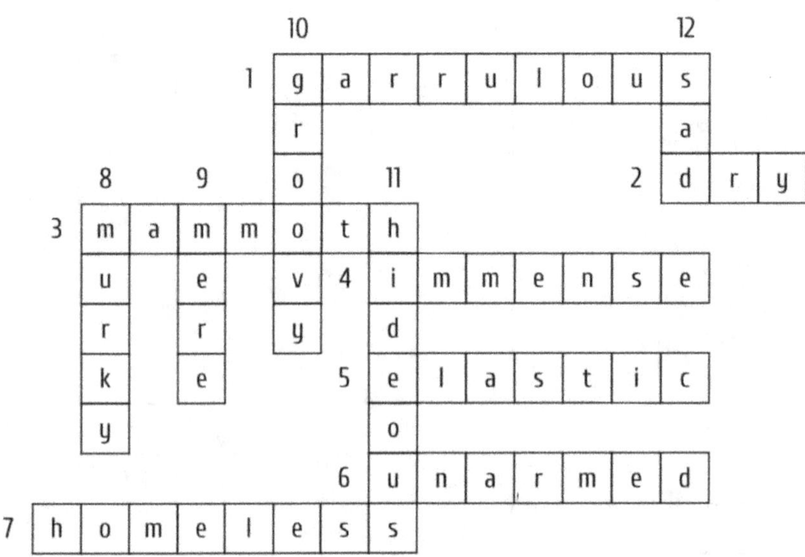

Across
1. Habit of talking a lot
2. No water or other liquid in
3. Gigantic prehistoric animal
4. Extremely large
5. Able to stretch
6. Not armed
7. Without a home

Down
8. Dark and dirty or difficult to see through
9. Nothing more than
10. Fashionable and interesting
11. Extremely ugly or bad
12. Unhappy or sorry

Across

1. Worried, nervous
2. Not in danger or likely to be harmed
3. Strong and unlikely to break or fail
4. Losing against someone
5. Said or thought by some people to be the stated bad or illegal thing, although you have no proof
6. Relating to love or a close loving relationship
7. Large in size or amount

Down

8. Happening or done quickly and without warning
9. Coming before all others
10. On or onto a ship, aircraft, bus, or train
11. Accepted, accept something
12. Respecting God
13. Boring
14. Containing, tasting of, or similar to nuts

Puzzle-28

Puzzle-28

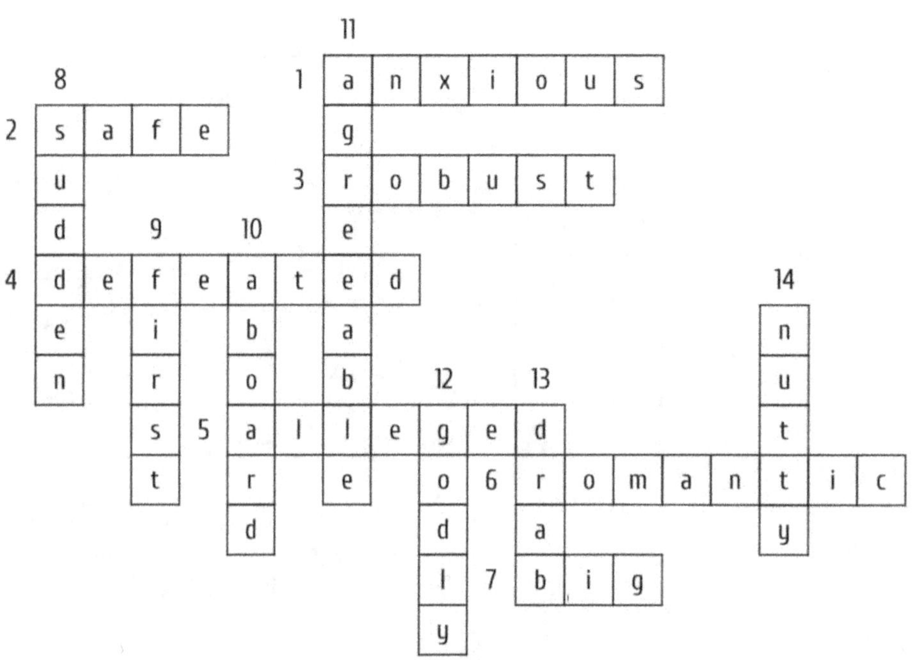

Across

1. Worried, nervous
2. Not in danger or likely to be harmed
3. Strong and unlikely to break or fail
4. Losing against someone
5. Said or thought by some people to be the stated bad or illegal thing, although you have no proof
6. Relating to love or a close loving relationship
7. Large in size or amount

Down

8. Happening or done quickly and without warning
9. Coming before all others
10. On or onto a ship, aircraft, bus, or train
11. Accepted, accept something
12. Respecting God
13. Boring
14. Containing, tasting of, or similar to nuts

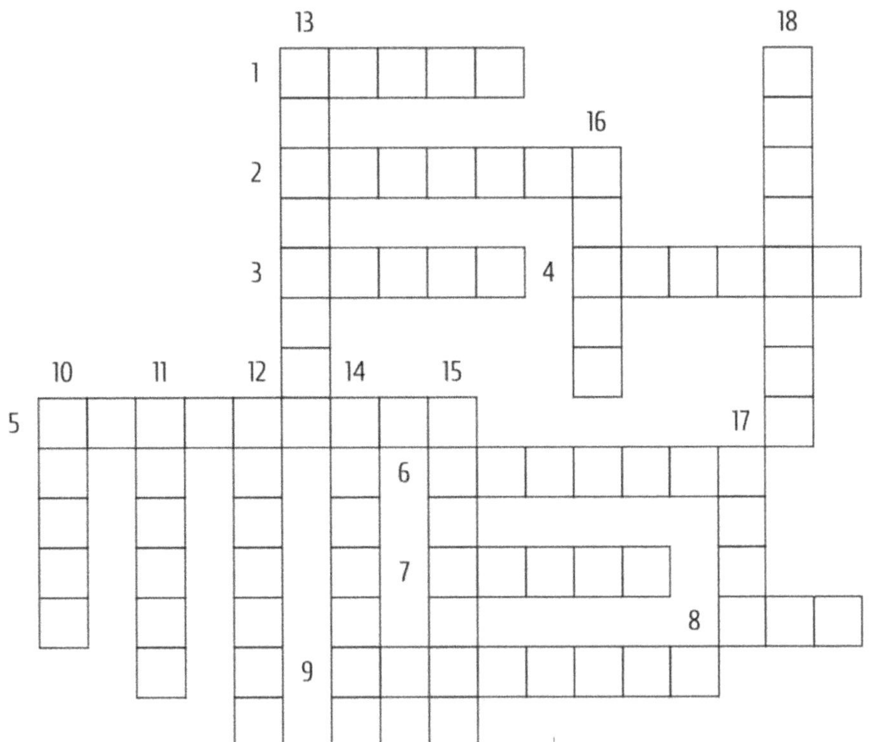

Across

1. Unkind, cruel
2. Gigantic prehistoric animal
3. Telling not the true
4. On or onto a ship, aircraft, bus, or train
5. Limited to only one person
6. Showing much knowledge
7. Respecting God
8. Unpleasant and causing difficulties or harm, evil, low quality, not acceptable
9. Not guilty of aparticular crime

Down

10. Develop
11. With clouds
12. Not armed
13. Without a home
14. A foolish idea
15. Attractive in appearance
16. Feel slightly drunk
17. Boring
18. Abnormal, deviant, different

Puzzle-29

Puzzle-29

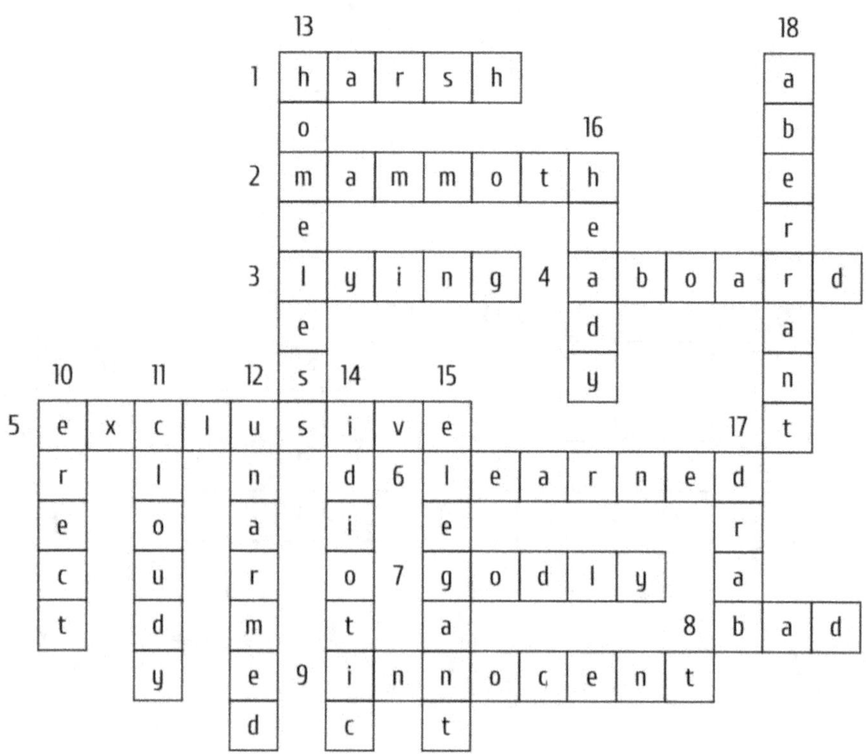

Across
1. Unkind, cruel
2. Gigantic prehistoric animal
3. Telling not the true
4. On or onto a ship, aircraft, bus, or train
5. Limited to only one person
6. Showing much knowledge
7. Respecting God
8. Unpleasant and causing difficulties or harm, evil, low quality, not acceptable
9. Not guilty of aparticular crime

Down
10. Develop
11. With clouds
12. Not armed
13. Without a home
14. A foolish idea
15. Attractive in appearance
16. Feel slightly drunk
17. Boring
18. Abnormal, deviant, different

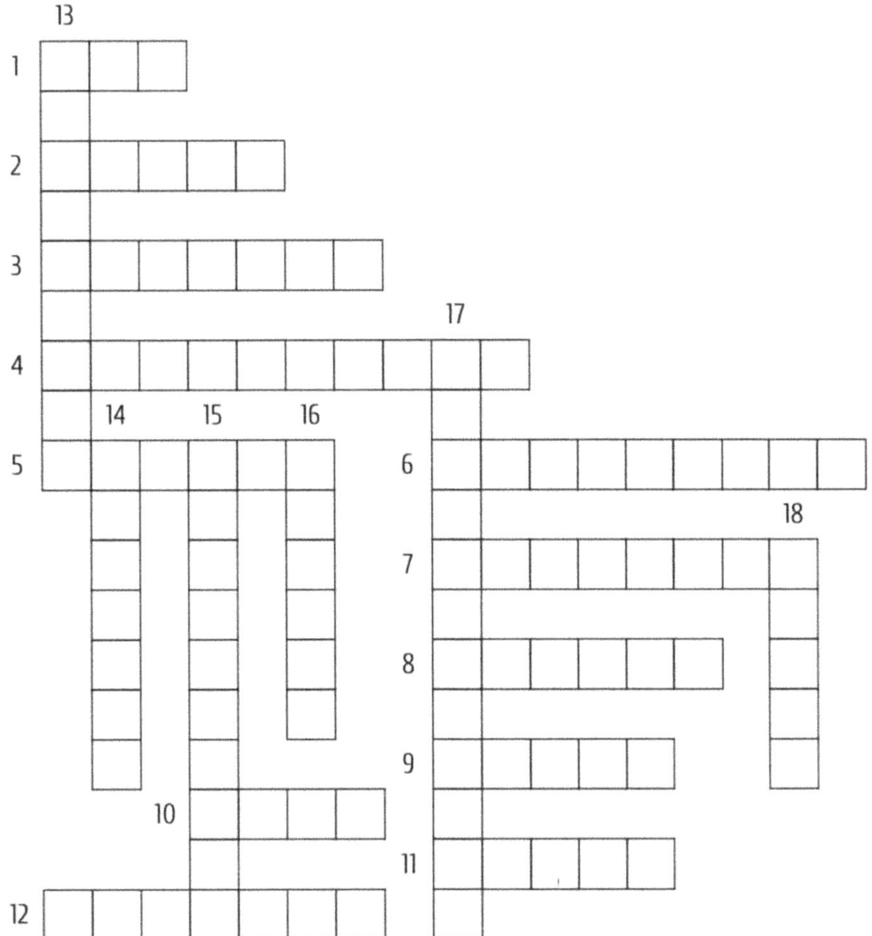

Across

1. No water or other liquid in
2. Containing, tasting of, or similar to nuts
3. Able to stretch
4. Unacceptable, offensive, violent, or unusual
5. Happening or done quickly and without warning
6. Gradually and secretly causing harm
7. Happy or grateful because of something
8. Strong and unlikely to break or fail
9. Not bitter or salty
10. Level and smooth
11. Develop
12. Unkind, cruel, without sympathy

Down

13. Hing, or activity could harm you
14. Not armed
15. Very pleasant
16. Ordinary or usual
17. Not excited
18. At the same height

Puzzle-30

Puzzle-30

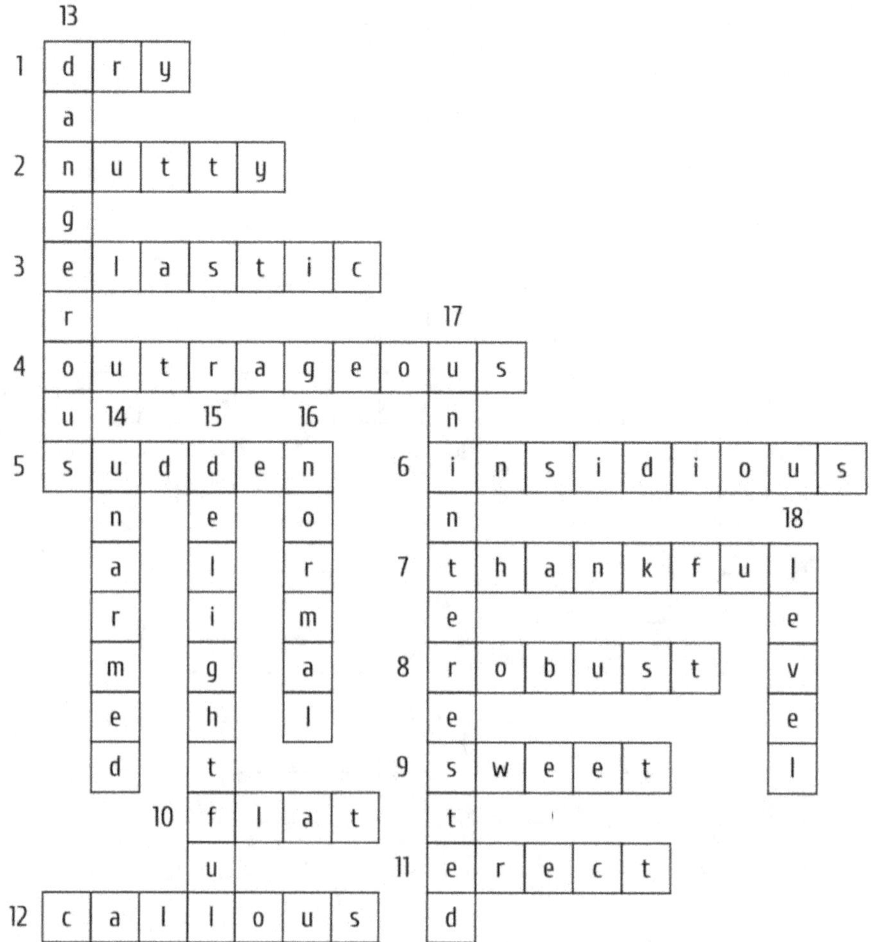

Across
1. No water or other liquid in
2. Containing, tasting of, or similar to nuts
3. Able to stretch
4. Unacceptable, offensive, violent, or unusual
5. Happening or done quickly and without warning
6. Gradually and secretly causing harm
7. Happy or grateful because of something
8. Strong and unlikely to break or fail
9. Not bitter or salty
10. Level and smooth
11. Develop
12. Unkind, cruel, without sympathy

Down
13. Hing, or activity could harm you
14. Not armed
15. Very pleasant
16. Ordinary or usual
17. Not excited
18. At the same height

Across

1. Complicated and difficult to solve
2. Hard or firm
3. Develop
4. Careful not to attract too much attention
5. Poor, unsuccessful, the state of being extremely unhappy
6. Boring
7. Unhappy or sorry
8. Able to stretch

Down

9. Harmed or spoiled
10. Not wanting others to know
11. Habit of talking a lot
12. Rightened or worried
13. Revealing
14. Losing against someone
15. Shaped like a ball or circle
16. Unpleasant and causing difficulties or harm, evil, low quality, not acceptable
17. Containing, tasting of, or similar to nuts
18. Attractive or pleasant

Puzzle-31

Puzzle-31

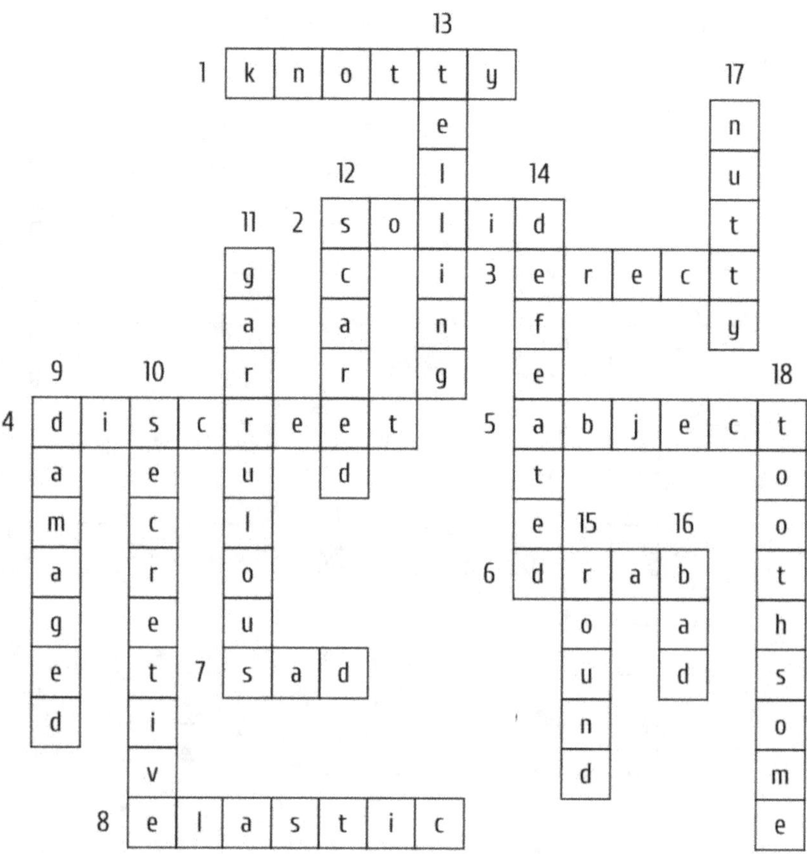

Across
1. Complicated and difficult to solve
2. Hard or firm
3. Develop
4. Careful not to attract too much attention
5. Poor, unsuccessful, the state of being extremely unhappy
6. Boring
7. Unhappy or sorry
8. Able to stretch

Down
9. Harmed or spoiled
10. Not wanting others to know
11. Habit of talking a lot
12. Rightened or worried
13. Revealing
14. Losing against someone
15. Shaped like a ball or circle
16. Unpleasant and causing difficulties or harm, evil, low quality, not acceptable
17. Containing, tasting of, or similar to nuts
18. Attractive or pleasant

Across

1. Dark and dirty or difficult to see through
2. Officer
3. Attractive or pleasant
4. Unacceptable, offensive, violent, or unusual
5. Rightened or worried
6. Loved very much
7. Coming before all others
8. Worried, nervous
9. Happy or grateful because of something
10. Revealing

Down

11. Beautiful, powerful, or causing great admiration and respect
12. Not bitter or salty
13. Morally correct
14. Happy and positive
15. Strong and unlikely to break or fail
16. Refusing to obey
17. Unhappy or sorry
18. Abnormal, deviant, different

Puzzle-32

Puzzle-32

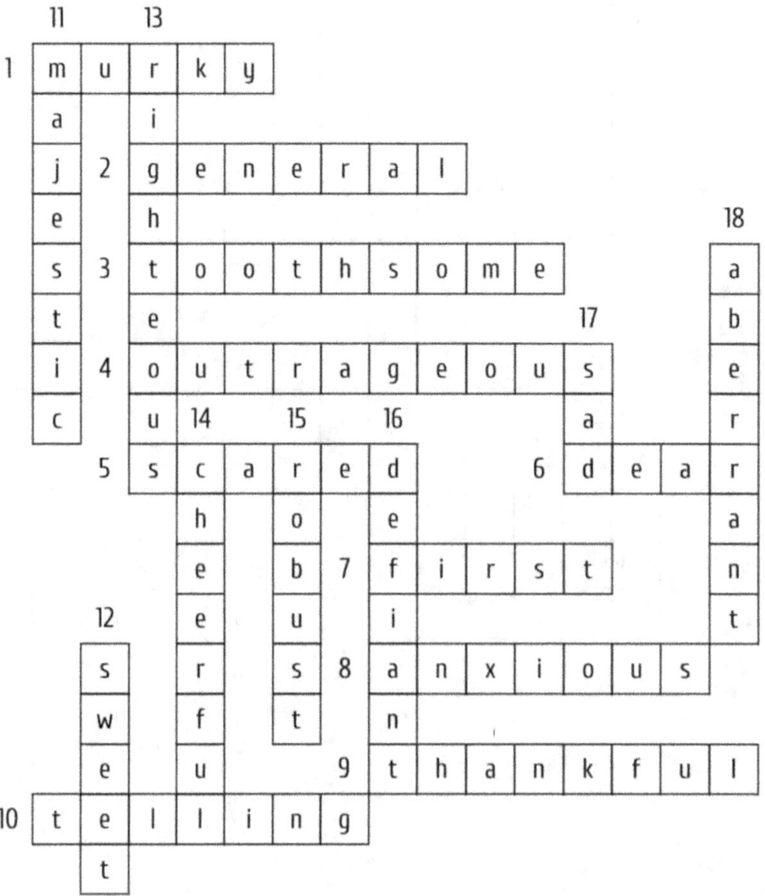

Across
1. Dark and dirty or difficult to see through
2. Officer
3. Attractive or pleasant
4. Unacceptable, offensive, violent, or unusual
5. Rightened or worried
6. Loved very much
7. Coming before all others
8. Worried, nervous
9. Happy or grateful because of something
10. Revealing

Down
11. Beautiful, powerful, or causing great admiration and respect
12. Not bitter or salty
13. Morally correct
14. Happy and positive
15. Strong and unlikely to break or fail
16. Refusing to obey
17. Unhappy or sorry
18. Abnormal, deviant, different

Across

1. Not dirty
2. Detestable, repugnant, repulsive, morally very bad
3. A foolish idea
4. Immediately after the first and before any others
5. Unwilling to give information
6. Not far away in distance

Down

7. Not in danger or likely to be harmed
8. Full of people
9. Rounded in a pleasant and attractive way
10. Not guilty of aparticular crime
11. Fashionable and interesting
12. Avoids risks

Puzzle-33

Puzzle-33

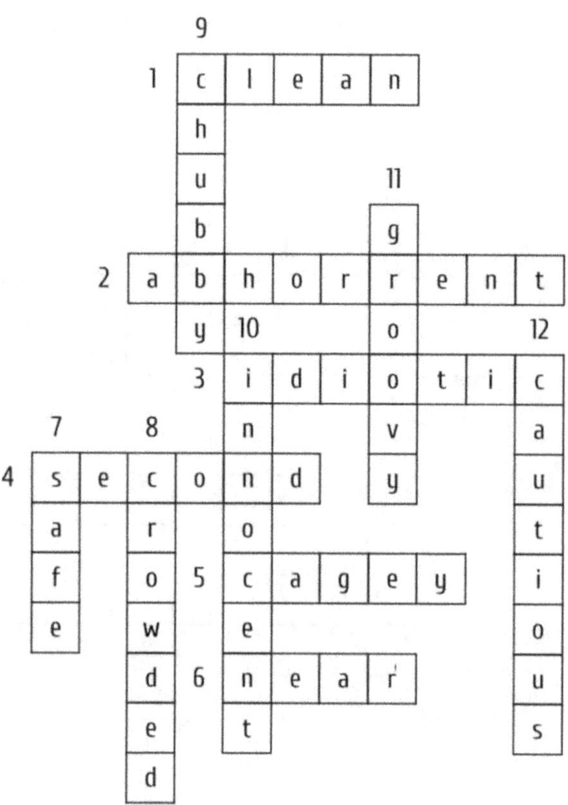

Across
1. Not dirty
2. Detestable, repugnant, repulsive, morally very bad
3. A foolish idea
4. Immediately after the first and before any others
5. Unwilling to give information
6. Not far away in distance

Down
7. Not in danger or likely to be harmed
8. Full of people
9. Rounded in a pleasant and attractive way
10. Not guilty of aparticular crime
11. Fashionable and interesting
12. Avoids risks

Across

1. Shaped like a ball or circle
2. Expressing thanks
3. Revealing
4. Fashionable and interesting
5. Not difficult
6. No water or other liquid in
7. Not bitter or salty
8. Said or thought by some people to be the stated bad or illegal thing, although you have no proof

Down

9. Not physically strong
10. Grand very large
11. Morally correct
12. Extremely large
13. Having a lot of power to control people and events
14. Able to stretch

Puzzle-34

Puzzle-34

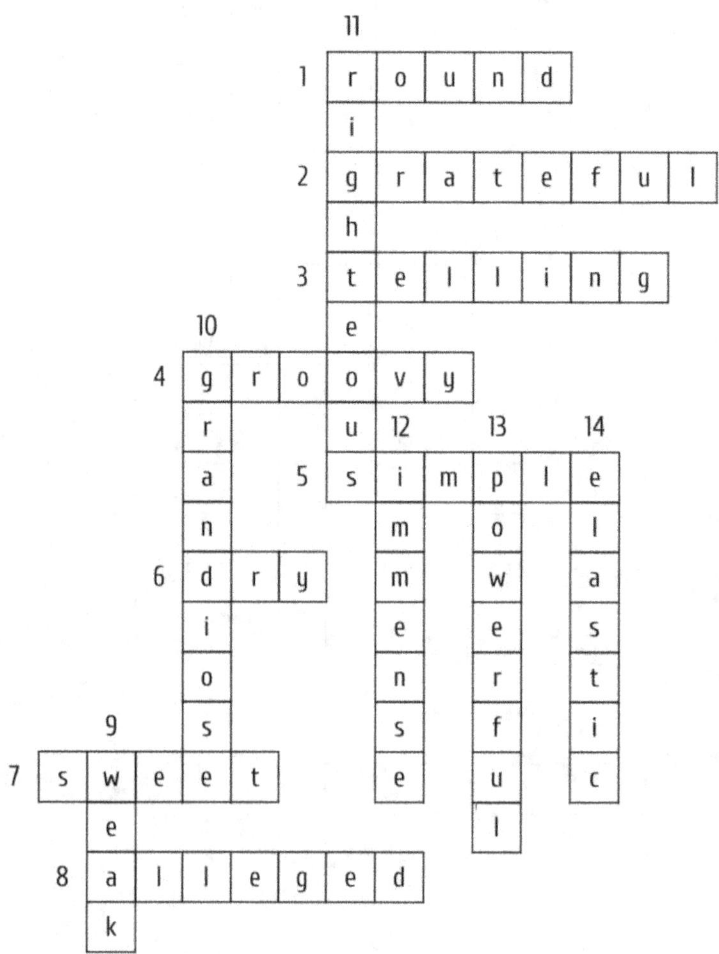

Across
1. Shaped like a ball or circle
2. Expressing thanks
3. Revealing
4. Fashionable and interesting
5. Not difficult
6. No water or other liquid in
7. Not bitter or salty
8. Said or thought by some people to be the stated bad or illegal thing, although you have no proof

Down
9. Not physically strong
10. Grand very large
11. Morally correct
12. Extremely large
13. Having a lot of power to control people and events
14. Able to stretch

Across

1. Not far away in distance
2. Expressing thanks
3. Extremely ugly or bad
4. Limited to only one person
5. Develop
6. Attractive or pleasant
7. Extremely large
8. Not bitter or salty

Down

9. Physically attractive
10. Loved very much
11. Fashionable and interesting
12. Intentionally choosing some things and not others
13. Containing, tasting of, or similar to nuts
14. Not in danger or likely to be harmed
15. Man
16. Careful not to attract too much attention

Puzzle-35

Puzzle-35

Across
1. Not far away in distance
2. Expressing thanks
3. Extremely ugly or bad
4. Limited to only one person
5. Develop
6. Attractive or pleasant
7. Extremely large
8. Not bitter or salty

Down
9. Physically attractive
10. Loved very much
11. Fashionable and interesting
12. Intentionally choosing some things and not others
13. Containing, tasting of, or similar to nuts
14. Not in danger or likely to be harmed
15. Man
16. Careful not to attract too much attention

Across

1. Poor, unsuccessful, the state of being extremely unhappy
2. Difficult to understand
3. Expressing thanks
4. Dissolves materials
5. Very pleasant
6. Not guilty of aparticular crime
7. Not physically strong
8. Loved very much
9. At the same height
10. Hard or firm

Down

11. With clouds
12. Beautiful, powerful, or causing great admiration and respect
13. Said or thought by some people to be the stated bad or illegal thing, although you have no proof
14. Containing, tasting of, or similar to nuts
15. Full of people
16. Not clear and having no form
17. Coming before all others
18. No water or other liquid in
19. Very respected
20. Attractive in appearance
21. Happening or done quickly and without warning
22. Shaped like a ball or circle

Puzzle-36

Puzzle-36

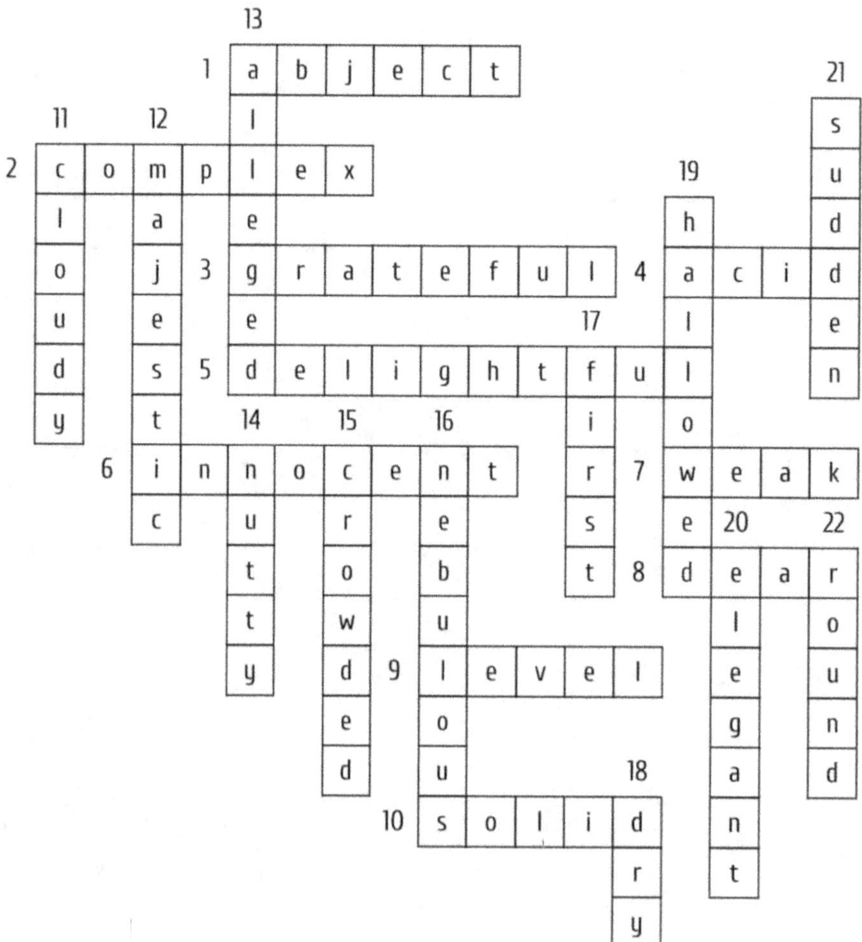

Across
1. Poor, unsuccessful, the state of being extremely unhappy
2. Difficult to understand
3. Expressing thanks
4. Dissolves materials
5. Very pleasant
6. Not guilty of aparticular crime
7. Not physically strong
8. Loved very much
9. At the same height
10. Hard or firm

Down
11. With clouds
12. Beautiful, powerful, or causing great admiration and respect
13. Said or thought by some people to be the stated bad or illegal thing, although you have no proof
14. Containing, tasting of, or similar to nuts
15. Full of people
16. Not clear and having no form
17. Coming before all others
18. No water or other liquid in
19. Very respected
20. Attractive in appearance
21. Happening or done quickly and without warning
22. Shaped like a ball or circle

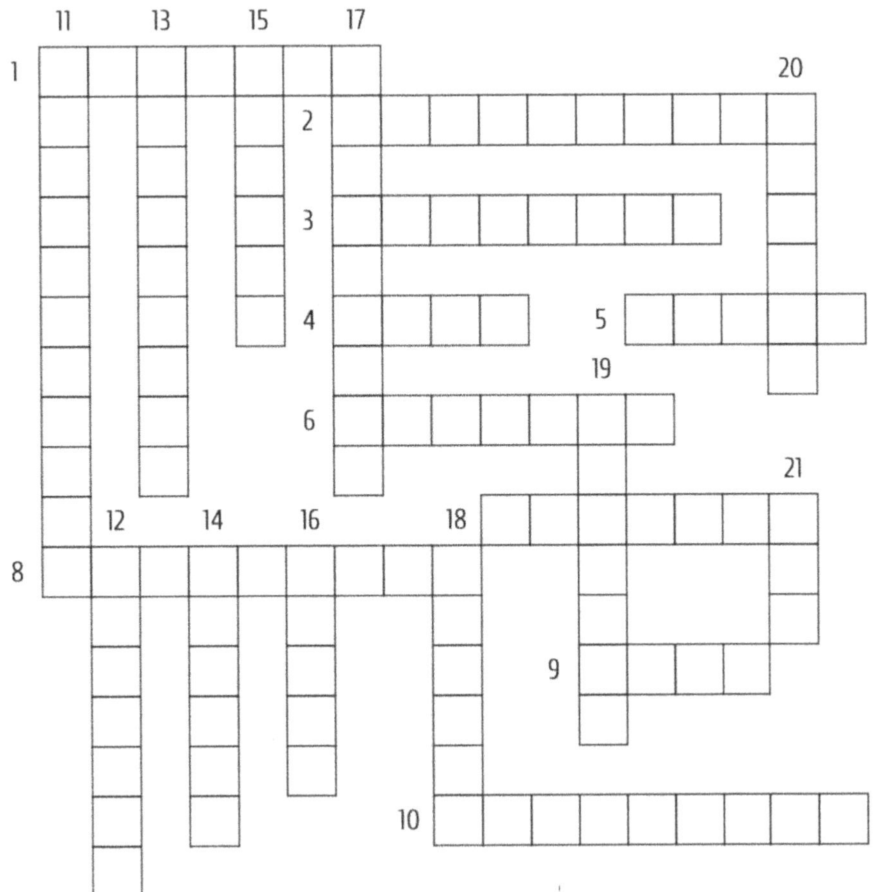

Across

1. Attractive in appearance
2. Unacceptable, offensive, violent, or unusual
3. Happy or grateful because of something
4. Not in danger or likely to be harmed
5. Not bitter or salty
6. Gigantic prehistoric animal
7. Said or thought by some people to be the stated bad or illegal thing, although you have no proof
8. Habit of talking a lot
9. Not far away in distance
10. Limited to only one person

Down

11. Make something more likely to happen
12. Worried, nervous
13. Having a lot of energy
14. Strong and unlikely to break or fail
15. Poor, unsuccessful, the state of being extremely unhappy
16. Telling not the true
17. Attractive or pleasant
18. Not difficult
19. Revealing
20. Rightened or worried
21. No water or other liquid in

Puzzle-37

Puzzle-37

Across
1. Attractive in appearance
2. Unacceptable, offensive, violent, or unusual
3. Happy or grateful because of something
4. Not in danger or likely to be harmed
5. Not bitter or salty
6. Gigantic prehistoric animal
7. Said or thought by some people to be the stated bad or illegal thing, although you have no proof
8. Habit of talking a lot
9. Not far away in distance
10. Limited to only one person

Down
11. Make something more likely to happen
12. Worried, nervous
13. Having a lot of energy
14. Strong and unlikely to break or fail
15. Poor, unsuccessful, the state of being extremely unhappy
16. Telling not the true
17. Attractive or pleasant
18. Not difficult
19. Revealing
20. Rightened or worried
21. No water or other liquid in

Across

1. Unkind, cruel
2. Containing, tasting of, or similar to nuts
3. Strong and unlikely to break or fail
4. Careful not to attract too much attention
5. Develop
6. Able to produce the intended result
7. Ability to do an activity or job well

Down

8. Happening or done quickly and without warning
9. Without a home
10. Happy and positive
11. Shaped like a ball or circle
12. Not armed
13. Not in danger or likely to be harmed
14. Unhappy or sorry

Puzzle-38

Puzzle-38

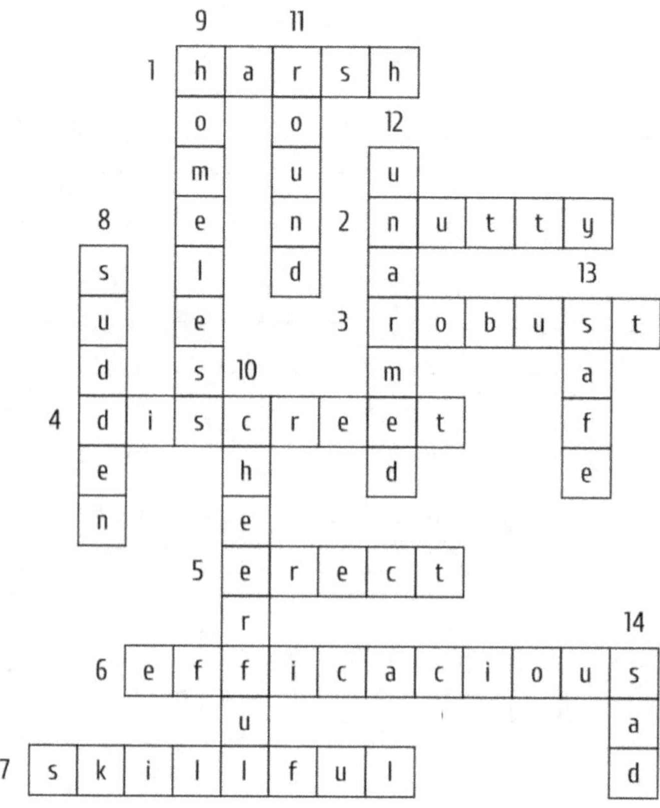

Across
1. Unkind, cruel
2. Containing, tasting of, or similar to nuts
3. Strong and unlikely to break or fail
4. Careful not to attract too much attention
5. Develop
6. Able to produce the intended result
7. Ability to do an activity or job well

Down
8. Happening or done quickly and without warning
9. Without a home
10. Happy and positive
11. Shaped like a ball or circle
12. Not armed
13. Not in danger or likely to be harmed
14. Unhappy or sorry

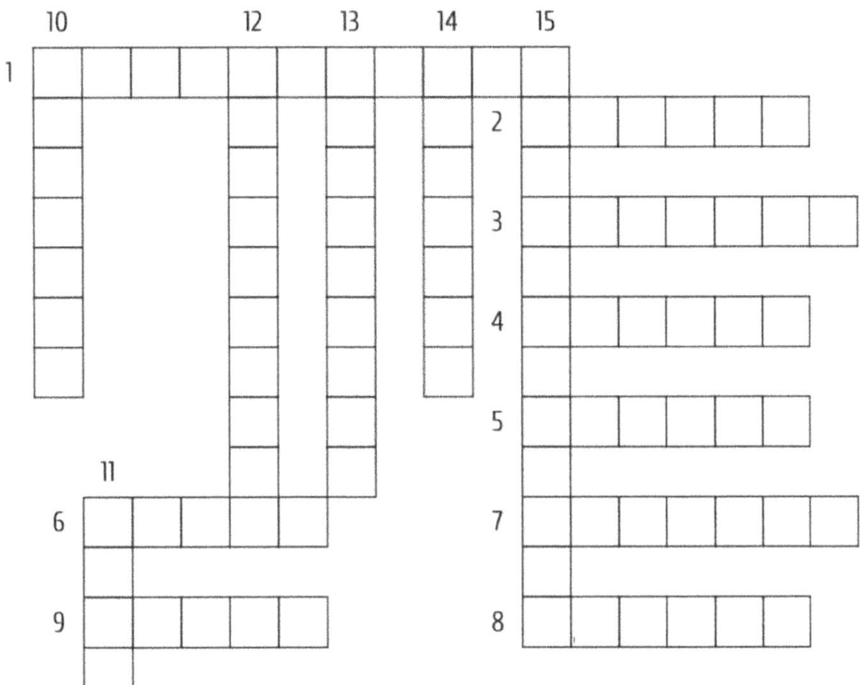

Across

1. Eager to know a lot
2. Ordinary or usual
3. Stopping and starting repeatedly
4. Immediately after the first and before any others
5. On or onto a ship, aircraft, bus, or train
6. Not bitter or salty
7. Revealing
8. Rounded in a pleasant and attractive way
9. Coming before all others

Down

10. A foolish idea
11. Not in danger or likely to be harmed
12. Impossible to defeat
13. Gradually and secretly causing harm
14. Extremely large
15. Feeling of energetic interest

Puzzle-39

Puzzle-39

Across
1. Eager to know a lot
2. Ordinary or usual
3. Stopping and starting repeatedly
4. Immediately after the first and before any others
5. On or onto a ship, aircraft, bus, or train
6. Not bitter or salty
7. Revealing
8. Rounded in a pleasant and attractive way
9. Coming before all others

Down
10. A foolish idea
11. Not in danger or likely to be harmed
12. Impossible to defeat
13. Gradually and secretly causing harm
14. Extremely large
15. Feeling of energetic interest

Across

1. Not the same
2. Strong and unlikely to break or fail
3. Accepted, accept something
4. Coming before all others
5. Very respected

Down

6. Dissolves materials
7. No water or other liquid in
8. Unkind, cruel
9. At the same height
10. Often forgetting things
11. Not physically strong
12. Loved very much

Puzzle-40

Puzzle-40

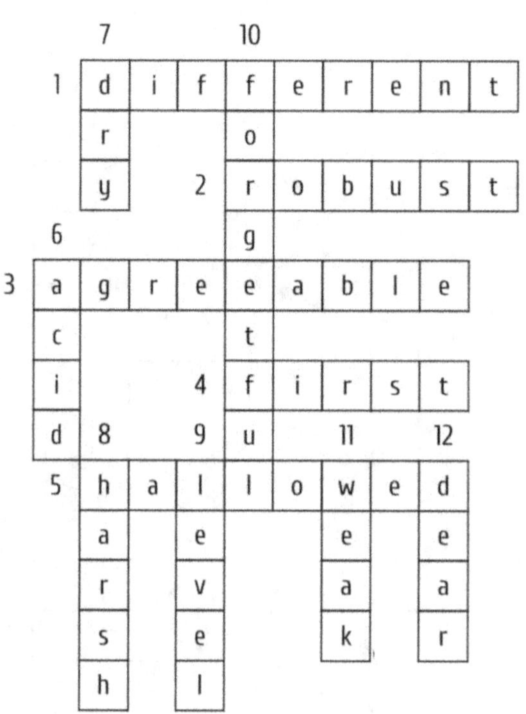

Across
1. Not the same
2. Strong and unlikely to break or fail
3. Accepted, accept something
4. Coming before all others
5. Very respected

Down
6. Dissolves materials
7. No water or other liquid in
8. Unkind, cruel
9. At the same height
10. Often forgetting things
11. Not physically strong
12. Loved very much

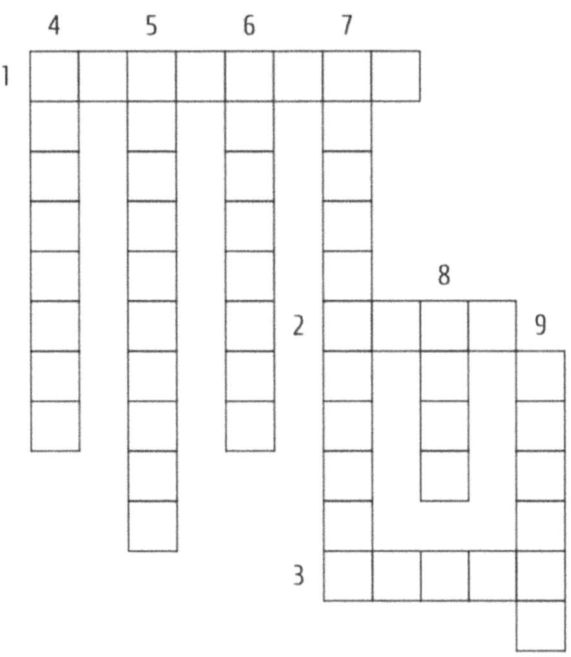

Across

1. Having a pleasant smell
2. Not in danger or likely to be harmed
3. Develop

Down

4. Excited, interested, enthusiastic
5. Unacceptable, offensive, violent, or unusual
6. Abnormal, deviant, different
7. Eager to know a lot
8. Level and smooth
9. Complicated and difficult to solve

Puzzle-41

Puzzle-41

Across
1. Having a pleasant smell
2. Not in danger or likely to be harmed
3. Develop

Down
4. Excited, interested, enthusiastic
5. Unacceptable, offensive, violent, or unusual
6. Abnormal, deviant, different
7. Eager to know a lot
8. Level and smooth
9. Complicated and difficult to solve

Across
1. Not in danger or likely to be harmed
2. No water or other liquid in
3. Not dirty
4. Broken part
5. Strong and unlikely to break or fail
6. At the same height
7. Avoids risks

Down
8. Drinking too much alcohol
9. Not the same
10. Fact that everyone knows
11. A foolish idea
12. Happy and positive
13. Not bitter or salty
14. Containing, tasting of, or similar to nuts

Puzzle-42

Puzzle-42

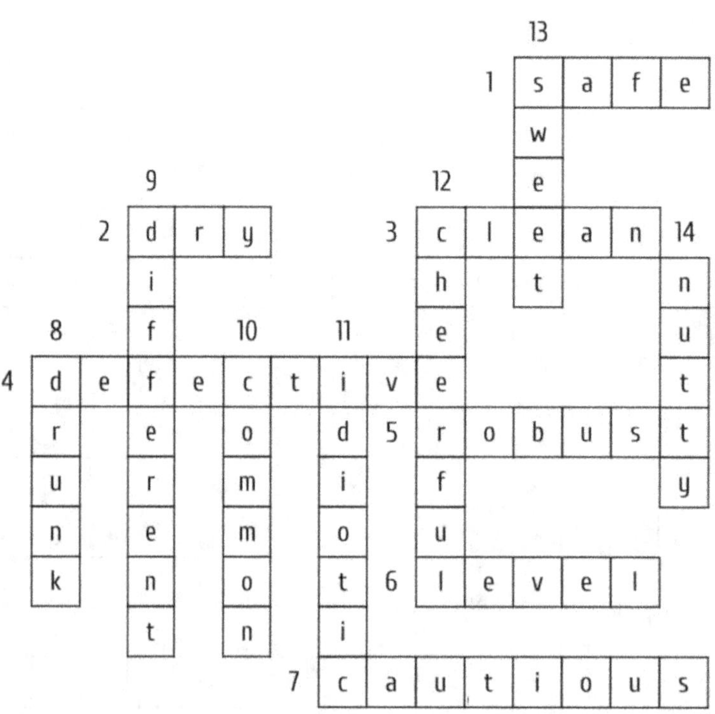

Across
1. Not in danger or likely to be harmed
2. No water or other liquid in
3. Not dirty
4. Broken part
5. Strong and unlikely to break or fail
6. At the same height
7. Avoids risks

Down
8. Drinking too much alcohol
9. Not the same
10. Fact that everyone knows
11. A foolish idea
12. Happy and positive
13. Not bitter or salty
14. Containing, tasting of, or similar to nuts

Across

1. Not in danger or likely to be harmed
2. Clever
3. Extremely large
4. Able to be obtained, used, or reached
5. No water or other liquid in
6. Abnormal, deviant, different
7. Containing, tasting of, or similar to nuts
8. Extremely cold

Down

9. Damaged
10. Stupid,unreasonable, silly in a humorous way, things that happen that are unreasonable
11. On or onto a ship, aircraft, bus, or train
12. Not far away in distance
13. Develop
14. Detestable, repugnant, repulsive, morally very bad
15. Ability to do an activity or job well
16. The color of chocolate
17. Having a lot of energy
18. Attractive in appearance

Puzzle-43

Puzzle-43

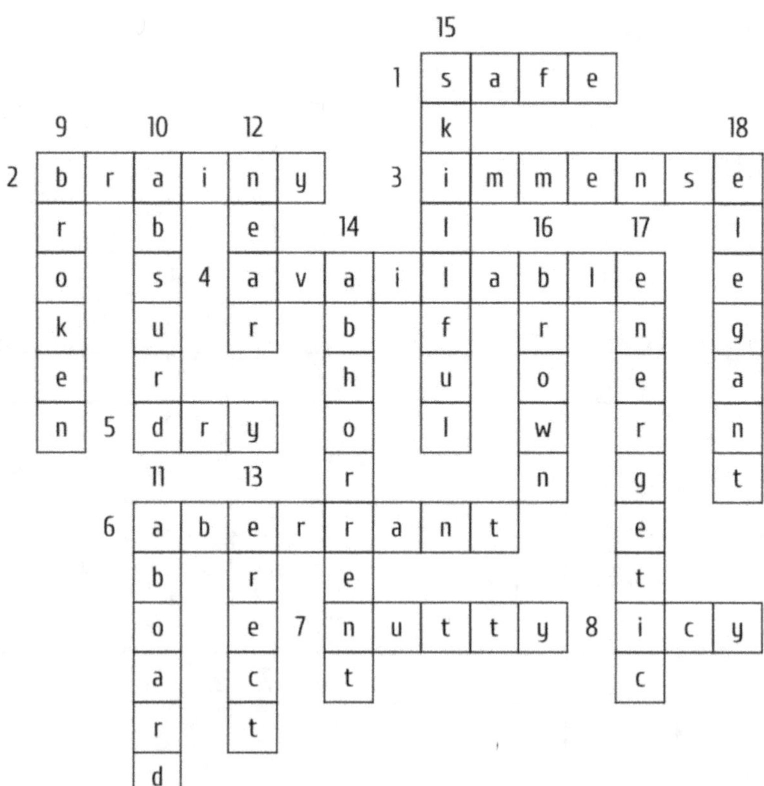

Across
1. Not in danger or likely to be harmed
2. Clever
3. Extremely large
4. Able to be obtained, used, or reached
5. No water or other liquid in
6. Abnormal, deviant, different
7. Containing, tasting of, or similar to nuts
8. Extremely cold

Down
9. Damaged
10. Stupid,unreasonable, silly in a humorous way, things that happen that are unreasonable
11. On or onto a ship, aircraft, bus, or train
12. Not far away in distance
13. Develop
14. Detestable, repugnant, repulsive, morally very bad
15. Ability to do an activity or job well
16. The color of chocolate
17. Having a lot of energy
18. Attractive in appearance

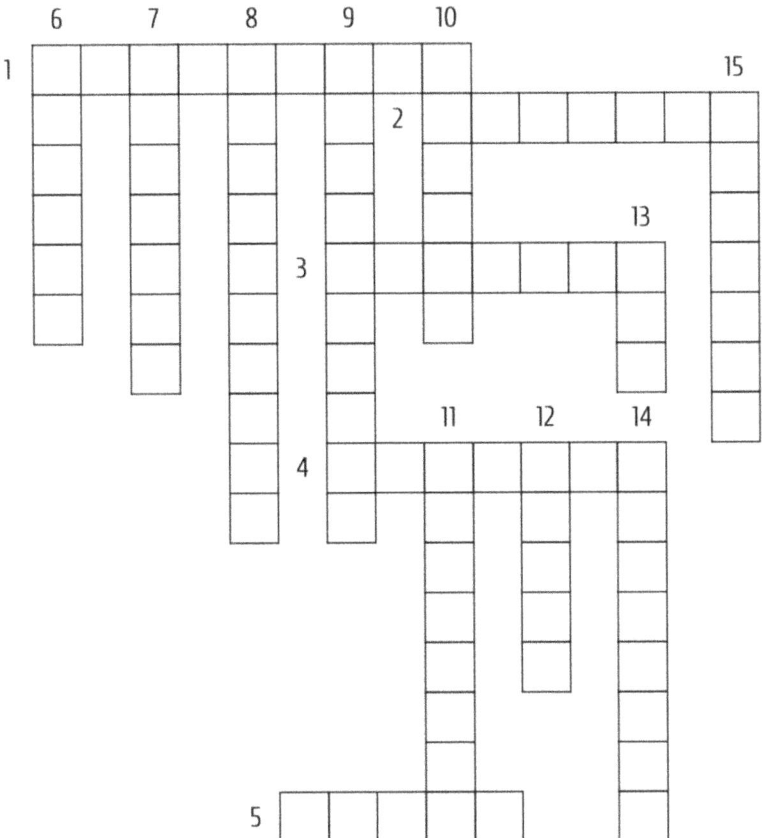

Across

1. Extremely funny
2. A foolish idea
3. Said or thought by some people to be the stated bad or illegal thing, although you have no proof
4. Not armed
5. Not bitter or salty

Down

6. Ordinary
7. Showing much knowledge
8. Able to send back light a surface
9. Unacceptable, offensive, violent, or unusual
10. Not difficult
11. Glue
12. Dark and dirty or difficult to see through
13. No water or other liquid in
14. Careful not to attract too much attention
15. Full of people

Puzzle-44

Puzzle-44

Across
1. Extremely funny
2. A foolish idea
3. Said or thought by some people to be the stated bad or illegal thing, although you have no proof
4. Not armed
5. Not bitter or salty

Down
6. Ordinary
7. Showing much knowledge
8. Able to send back light a surface
9. Unacceptable, offensive, violent, or unusual
10. Not difficult
11. Glue
12. Dark and dirty or difficult to see through
13. No water or other liquid in
14. Careful not to attract too much attention
15. Full of people

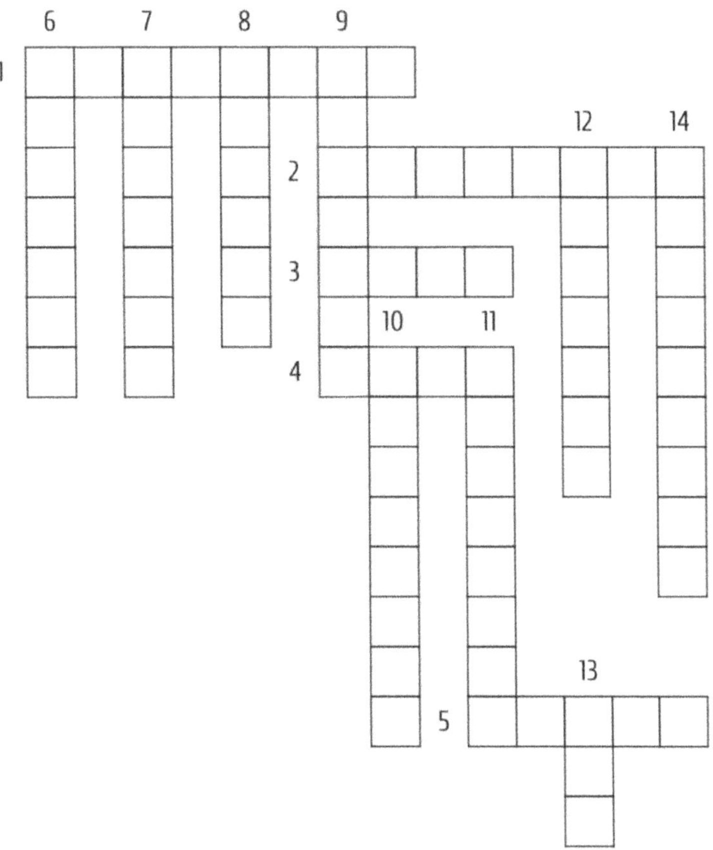

Across

1. Happy or grateful because of something
2. Abnormal, deviant, different
3. Man
4. Boring
5. Respecting God

Down

6. Revealing
7. Said or thought by some people to be the stated bad or illegal thing, although you have no proof
8. Complicated and difficult to solve
9. Not armed
10. Relating to love or a close loving relationship
11. Become pink in the face
12. Worried, nervous
13. No water or other liquid in
14. Attractive or pleasant

Puzzle-45

Puzzle-45

Across
1. Happy or grateful because of something
2. Abnormal, deviant, different
3. Man
4. Boring
5. Respecting God

Down
6. Revealing
7. Said or thought by some people to be the stated bad or illegal thing, although you have no proof
8. Complicated and difficult to solve
9. Not armed
10. Relating to love or a close loving relationship
11. Become pink in the face
12. Worried, nervous
13. No water or other liquid in
14. Attractive or pleasant

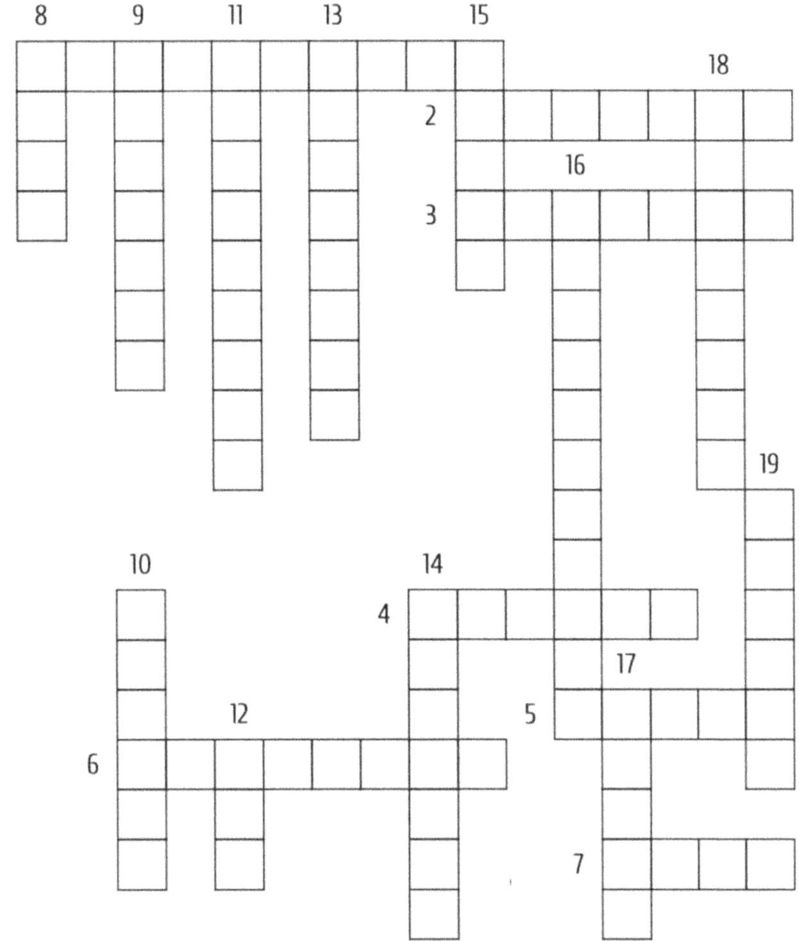

Across

1. Very pleasant
2. Able to stretch
3. Attractive in appearance
4. Fashionable and interesting
5. Not bitter or salty
6. Careful not to attract too much attention
7. Not far away in distance

Down

8. Loved very much
9. Showing much knowledge
10. Happening or done quickly and without warning
11. Habit of talking a lot
12. Unhappy or sorry
13. Happy or grateful because of something
14. Officer
15. At the same height
16. Able to produce the intended result
17. Not correct
18. Not guilty of aparticular crime
19. Complicated and difficult to solve

Puzzle-46

Puzzle-46

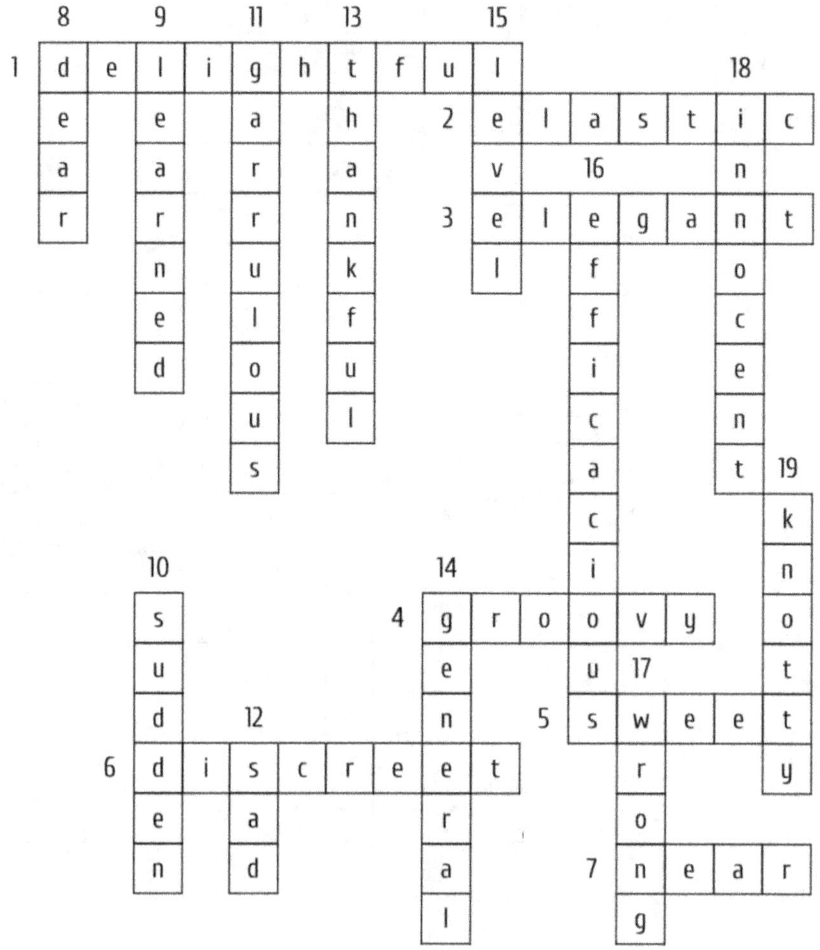

Across

1. Very pleasant
2. Able to stretch
3. Attractive in appearance
4. Fashionable and interesting
5. Not bitter or salty
6. Careful not to attract too much attention
7. Not far away in distance

Down

8. Loved very much
9. Showing much knowledge
10. Happening or done quickly and without warning
11. Habit of talking a lot
12. Unhappy or sorry
13. Happy or grateful because of something
14. Officer
15. At the same height
16. Able to produce the intended result
17. Not correct
18. Not guilty of aparticular crime
19. Complicated and difficult to solve

Across

1. Physically attractive
2. Fact that everyone knows
3. Containing, tasting of, or similar to nuts
4. Careful not to attract too much attention
5. Accepted, accept something
6. Drinking too much alcohol

Down

7. Easy to understand
8. Completely unable to think clearly or behave in a controlled way
9. Without a home
10. On or onto a ship, aircraft, bus, or train
11. Strong and unlikely to break or fail
12. Not excited

Puzzle-47

Puzzle-47

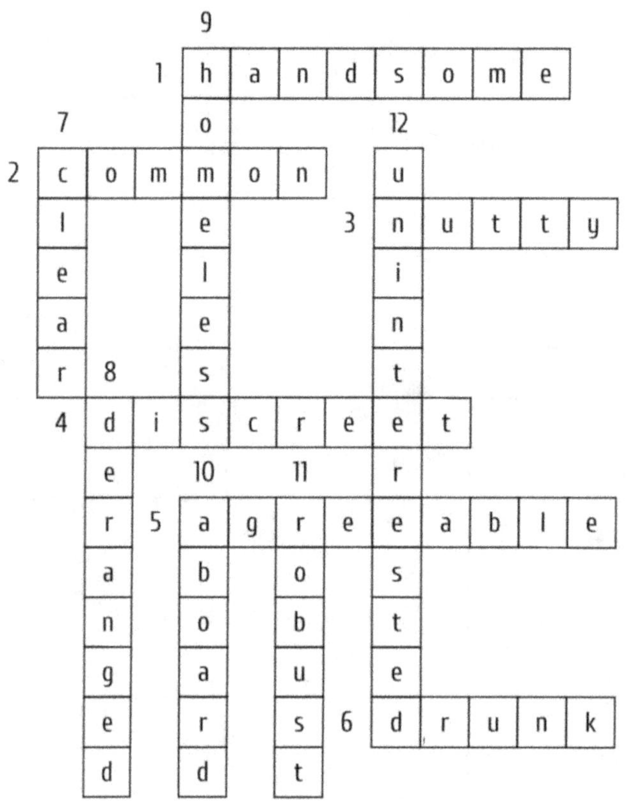

Across
1. Physically attractive
2. Fact that everyone knows
3. Containing, tasting of, or similar to nuts
4. Careful not to attract too much attention
5. Accepted, accept something
6. Drinking too much alcohol

Down
7. Easy to understand
8. Completely unable to think clearly or behave in a controlled way
9. Without a home
10. On or onto a ship, aircraft, bus, or train
11. Strong and unlikely to break or fail
12. Not excited

Across

1. Clever
2. Said or thought by some people to be the stated bad or illegal thing, although you have no proof
3. Respecting God
4. Abnormal, deviant, different
5. Not guilty of aparticular crime
6. Rounded in a pleasant and attractive way

Down

7. On or onto a ship, aircraft, bus, or train
8. Dissolves materials
9. A foolish idea
10. Disapproving, wishing to fight or argue
11. Large in size or amount
12. Easy to understand
13. Containing, tasting of, or similar to nuts

Puzzle-48

Puzzle-48

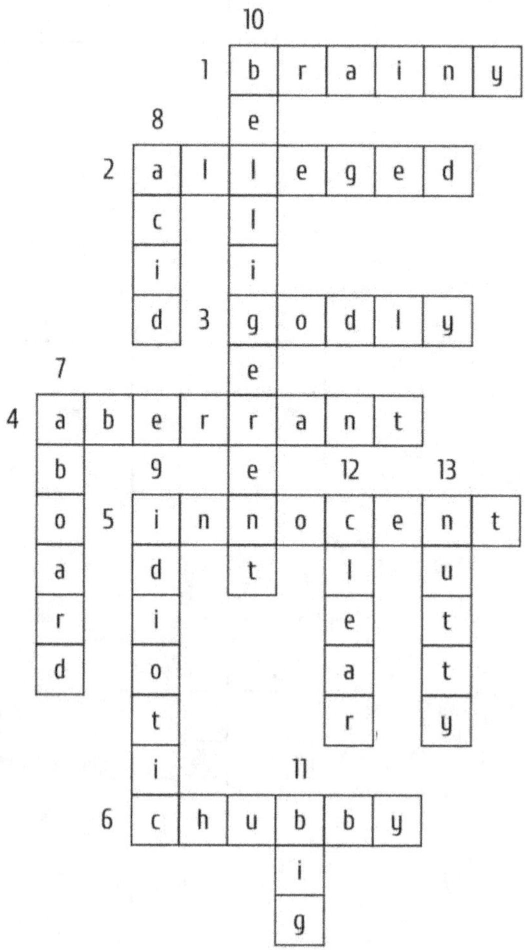

Across
1. Clever
2. Said or thought by some people to be the stated bad or illegal thing, although you have no proof
3. Respecting God
4. Abnormal, deviant, different
5. Not guilty of aparticular crime
6. Rounded in a pleasant and attractive way

Down
7. On or onto a ship, aircraft, bus, or train
8. Dissolves materials
9. A foolish idea
10. Disapproving, wishing to fight or argue
11. Large in size or amount
12. Easy to understand
13. Containing, tasting of, or similar to nuts

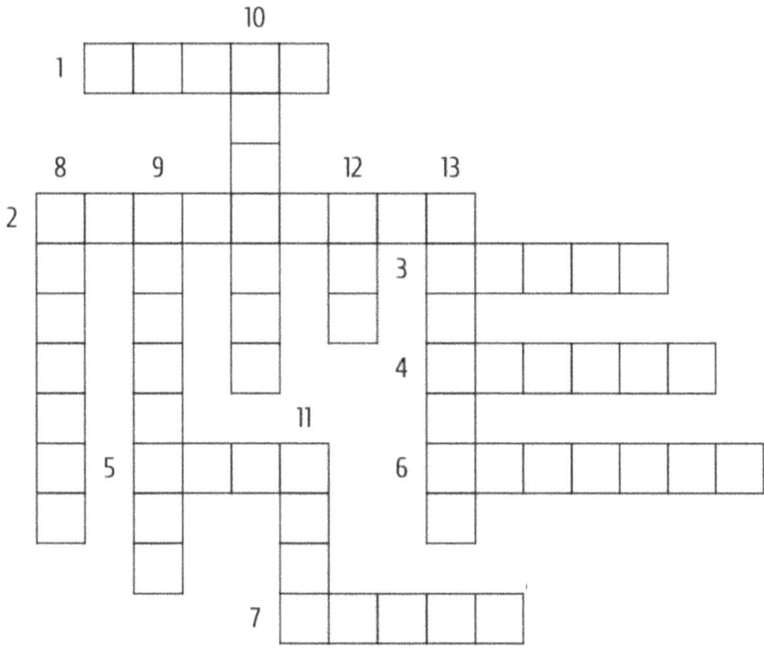

Across

1. Containing, tasting of, or similar to nuts
2. Able to be obtained, used, or reached
3. Telling not the true
4. Happening or done quickly and without warning
5. Dissolves materials
6. A foolish idea
7. Large and strong

Down

8. Said or thought by some people to be the stated bad or illegal thing, although you have no proof
9. Abnormal, deviant, different
10. Revealing
11. Boring
12. Large in size or amount
13. Able to stretch

Puzzle-49

Puzzle-49

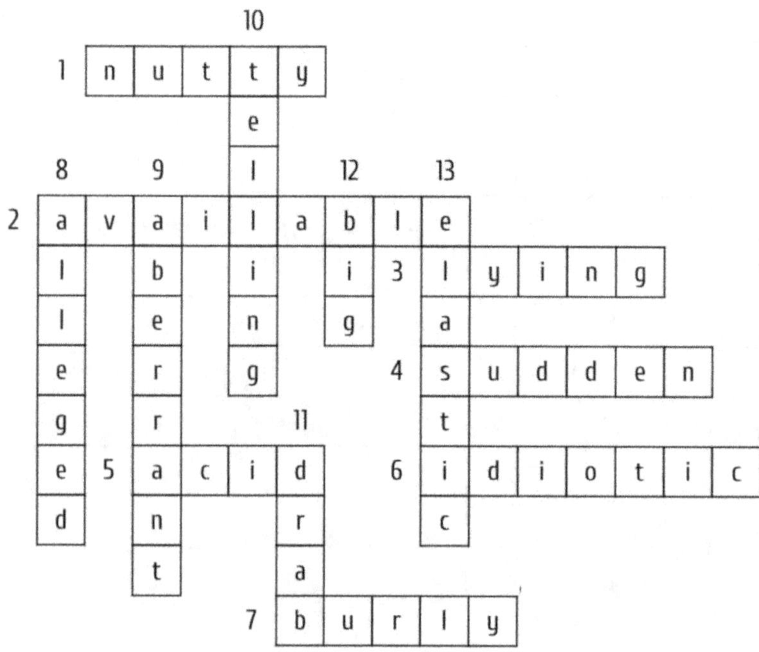

Across
1. Containing, tasting of, or similar to nuts
2. Able to be obtained, used, or reached
3. Telling not the true
4. Happening or done quickly and without warning
5. Dissolves materials
6. A foolish idea
7. Large and strong

Down
8. Said or thought by some people to be the stated bad or illegal thing, although you have no proof
9. Abnormal, deviant, different
10. Revealing
11. Boring
12. Large in size or amount
13. Able to stretch

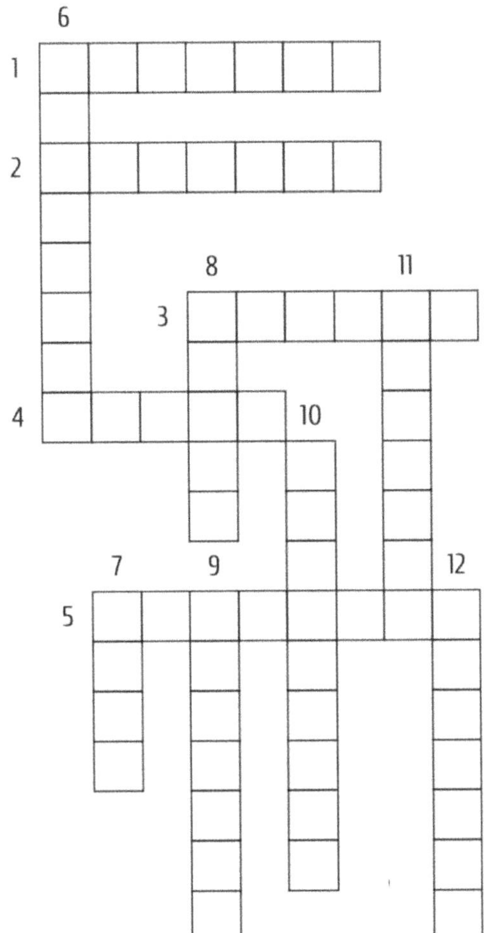

Across

1. Stopping and starting repeatedly
2. Gigantic prehistoric animal
3. Rounded in a pleasant and attractive way
4. Not bitter or salty
5. Careful not to attract too much attention

Down

6. Without a home
7. Boring
8. Easy to understand
9. Unusual and unexpected
10. Habit of talking a lot
11. Strange and unusual
12. Revealing

Puzzle-50

Puzzle-50

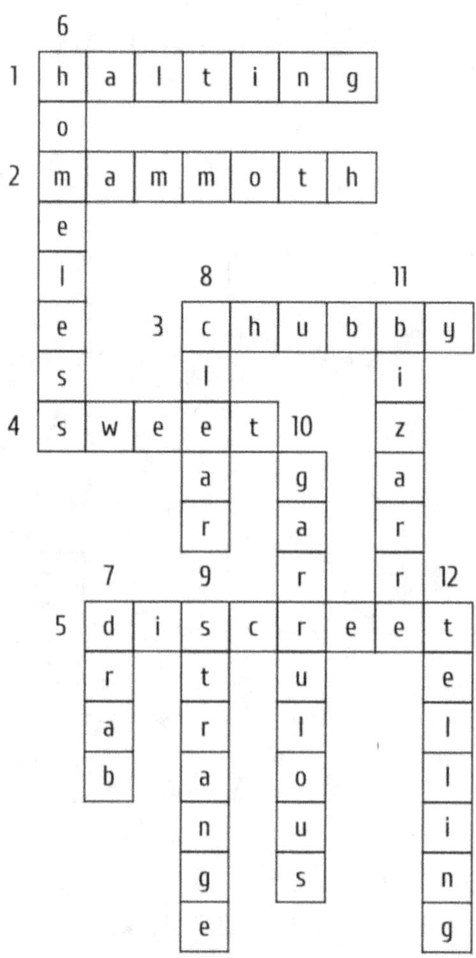

Across
1. Stopping and starting repeatedly
2. Gigantic prehistoric animal
3. Rounded in a pleasant and attractive way
4. Not bitter or salty
5. Careful not to attract too much attention

Down
6. Without a home
7. Boring
8. Easy to understand
9. Unusual and unexpected
10. Habit of talking a lot
11. Strange and unusual
12. Revealing